The Glory Hill Diaries

Maggie Barnes

ISBN (PRINT): 978-1-54398-461-3
ISBN (eBook): 978-1-54398-462-0

Acknowledgements

When it came to compiling this book, I was the original turtle on a fence post. I did not get here without help!

The seed of the idea came from the many local authors whose book signings and readings I attended. To a person, they were encouraging and told me to keep up with my writing. They helped me push past my hesitations about self-publishing and advocated for it as the next logical step. When no one laughed, I figured it was a good route to take.

Editing your own writing is mind numbing and dangerous. I needed a second pair of eyes I trusted to be the caretaker of my work. Never has there been a more delicate editor than Loren Penman. Several of these essays were expanded beyond their original manifestation and new ones were added. Her gentle guidance made the final product so much better than it would have been without her. Thanks, Boss.

Raphael Matigulin, my wonderful illustrator, was a joy to work with. He seemed to intuitively understand what I was after for each drawing. Calculating the time difference in London was a small price to pay to add his artistry to this collection. Let's do it again soon, my new friend.

Asking someone to take your photograph is an act of trust. Over the lifetime he and I have been friends, there has been a steadfast vow between Mark Webster and me that, should a day of publication ever come, he would take the cover photo and my author portrait for the back cover. There is no one I would have wanted more behind the lens.

Of course, without Mountain Home Magazine, there would have been nothing to compile! For reasons that continue to escape me,

Michael and Teresa Capuzzo saw something in my writing worth pursuing. They encouraged me, cheered me on, and trusted me with assignments that scared the hell out of me. I learned how to write much more than just my columns, as they let me profile world-famous musicians, get all-access passes to fascinating businesses, and shed tears over the stories people told me of their lives. They have celebrated every award with a confidence that spurned me onward. I offer this book as a gesture of thanks to them for giving my words their very first place to live.

It is only fitting that the person I owe the largest debt of thanks to is the most important person in my life. My husband, Robert, has put up with a lot in the quarter-century he has been married to me. But, for about three months in 2019, I really outdid myself in piling on the stress factors all at once. I had just started a job that returned me to a level of all-consuming involvement that we hadn't lived with for years. I was newly diagnosed with a life-long illness that would restructure many of our routines. Our youngest son was being deployed far from home. In the midst of this turmoil, I announced that I wanted to publish a collection of my essays. He would have been completely within his rights to have me committed. Instead, he said, "You should do it." Every time I had to shovel off the dining room table so we had somewhere to eat, every 5 a.m. he reached out, only to find me absent, every self-doubt I gave voice to – which was ALL of them – his affirmation of my abilities never wavered. No one deserves the kind of support he has always given me, but I accept it with deep thanks and spend each day trying to become the person he thinks I am. You are my heart, Bobby.

Introduction

"Are you a writer?"

Me? No. I handle a lot of communication needs for my employer. I write often, but always for other people. Letters that won't bear my signature, speeches I won't deliver, that sort of thing.

But I do love language. It's like music to me. People passing me on the highway must wonder, "Who the heck is she talking to?" I'm trying out sentences with different words and seeing how I can cram as much meaning into as few phrases as possible.

I have been blessed in that my life has provided me with numerous tales, most of them funny, about the ins and outs and ups and downs of everyday. Even the stuff that wasn't funny at the time got funny later. No matter what happens, if we can find something to laugh about, we're going to be fine.

One day, six years ago, a whole bunch of words were knocking at the back of my brain, trying to fall out of my head. So, I wrote them down. On a whim, I sent them to a woman I had recently met, a woman named Teresa Capuzzo. She, and her husband Michael, publish *Mountain Home Magazine* out of Wellsboro, Pennsylvania. We were kindred spirits in a way. Teresa loves language too, and adores a good story. That is part of the reason that the magazine morphed from a real estate publication into a monthly love letter about the region and its people.

I cannot tell you how close I came to not sending that first story. I had never written for publication before. I had no reason to think that what I had to say as a newcomer to the area was of interest to anyone. But I sent it anyway.

As they say, you often don't recognize the most significant moments while they are happening. Submitting that story changed my life. More than 50 appearances in *Mountain Home, Country Woman, Life in the Finger Lakes* and the guidebooks for Wellsboro, Bradford County and Route 6, and six state and national awards later, I cannot imagine my world without writing. It is an essential part of my happiness.

This compilation is another step in my journey towards finding out just how far my love of words can take me. You are now a part of that journey and I am eternally grateful for your support. I hope you find a smile or two in these pages.

See you on the hill!

Maggie Barnes
August, 2019
Glory Hill
Waverly, New York

Foreword

As the publisher of *Mountain Home* magazine, an award-winning monthly with 100,000 readers in the rural borderlands of New York and Pennsylvania, I've become accustomed to the question, "Can I submit something for publication?" The answer is a tricky one. *Mountain Home* is for everyone, "Free as the Wind" at hundreds of outlets—but not everyone can write for it. Eugene Roberts, the former managing editor of *The New York Times,* during whose tenure I worked when he was executive editor of *The Philadelphia Inquirer*, calls it, "brilliant journalism."

I'm picky.

But it was an especially delicate question coming from Maggie Barnes, a public relations associate for one of my most important clients, a major hospital to whom I was trying to sell an ad.

It was just a casual aside on her part, and of course I told her casually what I tell everyone: "We look at all stories we receive, so we'll be happy to take a look if you want to send something along." And then I had to tell her, with as much care and tact as I could summon, that the sales side and the writing side were completely different divisions (in spite of the fact that my name was at the top of both columns), so I could make no promises.

But after that first column came zinging into our mailbox a few months later, with a voice one part Erma Bombeck, one part Cathy Guisewite, and five parts pure Maggie, the only promise I needed to make was: please keep them coming and you are going to win some awards.

And that she did, one after another, as a columnist telling tales of the city girl moving to the country and her first encounter with a snake— in the *house*; or the yuletide bliss of trying to jam sixteen feet of Christmas tree into a twelve-foot-high living room; or the quiet realization that in a town so close that everyone knows everyone else's family (and everyone else's business) there is nonetheless a kind of lambent warmth in that fabric of life. Maggie aimed her pen at herself, wryly ambling through the trials and tribulations of life, from new hips, to new puppies, to learning to bake (it doesn't all end well…).

The Pennsylvania Newsmedia Association would end up awarding Maggie three first-place Keystone awards for column-writing in *Mountain Home*, and on the world stage (so far), she has won two IRMAs from the International Regional Magazine Association. Somewhere in there I thought to ask her how long she'd been writing before she submitted that initial column to us.

"Umm," she said, "That was the first one."

The Christmas after Maggie won her first Keystone award, a package came to the office addressed to me and Mike, my husband and co-publisher. In it was a child's wand, Disneyesque, glittery and magical. The Christmas card that came with it thanked us for tapping her and making her dreams come true, for making her what she had become—a writer.

That, of course, is not what happened. Someone a lot higher up had already done that. All we had to do was sit back and enjoy the read.

And now, it's your turn.

~ Teresa Banik Capuzzo
2 September 2019

New to the Hill

"Bobby? Why does this look like this?"

I am sure the confusion was evident in my voice as I stood in the bathroom, staring into the tub. My husband joined me and we peered into a bathtub of water the color of iced tea. That may have been the first time I felt like a stranger in a strange land in our new home, but it certainly wasn't the last.

We had been married for more than 16 years but had just bought our first home together in a region of southern New York and northern Pennsylvania commonly referred to as "The Valley." It was a unique house on a private dirt road – home to only three other families. And now we, town and city dwellers our whole lives, suddenly were perched on a hillside with five acres of land and new-to-us inventions like a septic tank and a well.

This returns us to the scene in the bathroom. Accustomed as I was to water the color of nothing, I was unprepared for the sight of a murky bath. It looked like a gang of golden retrievers had found a mud puddle, then dropped by to tell us about it. My husband, a highly capable individual with a 40-year career as an emergency manager, had a befuddled look on his face that mirrored mine.

"Maybe because it rained?" he offered. I could feel my eyebrows huddle together in the middle of my forehead as I thought. I turned back around to face the sink, filled a plastic cup from the faucet and stuck my nose into the glass. The same odd mix of water and brown met my sight. Tilting the cup so Bob could see it, I queried, "Is it going to do this every time it rains?" He had no reply.

It does. Every time we get an appreciable rainfall, the well water dons its tan. Our highly domesticated cats even back away from a water dish that looks like the remnants of dishwater. I have been reassured many times that there is nothing wrong with the water; it is just "roiled". Oh, that clears it up. My mind, that is-- nothing clears the water but time.

For our first Christmas here my sister bestowed upon us a book with a title she felt compelled to apologize for – *Country Living for Dummies*. We were not offended but relieved. A place to go for answers! All of which returns us to the bathroom on a night when the water was of bath quality. As I stepped out of it, my beloved appeared, carrying a plastic bucket and offering a wordless smile. He proceeded to scoop water from the tub with the bucket, walk across the bedroom out onto the upper deck and heave the contents of the bucket over the railing. Returning to the bathroom, he scooped again, gave me the same small smile and headed for the deck, being careful not to drip water on the finally installed carpet. A moment later came the sound of 2 1/2 gallons of liquid hitting the ground.

I leaned against the bathroom vanity and said nothing, mostly because I couldn't remember if it was sleepwalkers you weren't supposed to disturb or relocation-traumatized husbands who had clearly dropped a log or two from their mental woodpile.

On his fourth trip, the level of water in the tub dropping steadily, I risked a question.

"Babe? What in the name of sanity are you doing?"

Still scooping, he related that the *Country Living for Dummies* book specifically states that you should not empty the tub into the septic tank. When I followed that with the inevitable "Why not?" he paused, bent over the tub, bucket in mid-scoop.

"I don't know. But it's in the book."

The book has been very helpful, but the biggest repository of knowledge about living here is stored in the calendar, where the days and weeks have strung together like charms on a chain, each link carrying its own story. We are learning by living and working here, making discoveries and mistakes, new rules and old promises.

We are years into this adventure and, while we still qualify as "country living dummies," we no longer drain the bathtub with a bucket. We have survived the thunderstorms and winter attacks that

15

seem to vibrate the 15-foot windows in the living room. We have experienced that never-ending time known as "mud season" when nothing we own is clean – ever. We now know that we understood loose examples of "quiet" and "dark" before coming here, where you can literally hear your own heartbeat and bask in the complete absence of light.

As always, the challenges stand out – trying to get a level of technology into a house that has never known cable or Internet service. Accepting that people who move to a private road with four houses are probably not looking to get chummy with the new neighbors. Modernizing a home that looked like something out of a Doris Day/Rock Hudson movie.

But the truth is, even with the challenges, or maybe because of them, we count this time as one of the happiest of our lives. You haven't seen two people more in love with a house since the 2000 presidential election.

These are the stories of a husband, a wife, and the place that brought them a dream they didn't even know they had.

Pilgrims' Progress

"Should we try it?"

Bob and I were standing in front of a restaurant whose threshold we had never crossed, and I was having another one of my "stranger in a strange land" moments.

Changing communities brings a specific set of challenges. If you have lived in an area for many years, you take for granted that you know who has the best price on gas, who's open late which nights, and where you can get pizza you would cheerfully kill for. You know the roads that resemble Mt. Rainer when it snows and the routes of the school buses that are impossible to pass. Those without "local knowledge" have to rely on an odd combination of referral, luck, and the time-honored kindness of strangers. As a resident of "the Valley," a nebulous sort of location not found on a map, there are some hard and fast rules about traffic patterns and shopping habits that, if broken, really can tank a tightly planned agenda.

For instance, the concept of the three-way stop at a four-way intersection. These are normal looking four-way intersections, but only three of you have to stop. One gets a hall pass to slide on through. The first week I was working in Sayre I nearly got creamed

18

multiple times at corners where I would have bet the contents of my wallet that I had the right of way. I still can hear the conversation in my head: "Okay, I'm stopped. The person directly across from me is stopped. Here comes a car on my left. Naturally he is going to stop. So, forward I go and...*scrreeech! honnnk!* Hey! Why does he look so aggravated? He's the one who blew through the intersection!" I left a wake of confused and angry drivers waving at me (not using all the fingers God gave them, by the way) as I drove off, equally perturbed. Finally I caught on to these tripod points. The first time I waved a hesitant newbie through a three-way trap I felt very wise, like I had contributed rare wisdom to his life. Or kept him from getting broadsided, either one. Life is a series of small triumphs, people, take them where you find them!

One of the things that impressed us on our preliminary visit to the region was the number of small, independent businesses. "Mom and Pop" are still major players in the Valley economy, and we loved the

idea of supporting more than just corporations. Those of us still getting forwarded mail, however, are uneducated on things like the holiday shopping schedules of all our neighbors.

Our first December 31st, we thought that a couple of nice steaks would be the way to ring in the New Year. Moments later, I found myself in a tiny parking lot that was hosting a traffic jam. No one could move, but there was absolutely no stress or angst visible. In fact, people were chatting from car to car, mufflers filling the air with mist and windshield wipers slapping out happy tunes. Those who had managed to park were standing in the lanes exchanging holiday wishes with those inching past them. The meat counter was almost impenetrable, allowing me to develop an appreciation for the ballet-like movements of the staff as they doled out roasts, whole turkeys, and big smiles. Lesson learned. Now I go three days before the holiday and have entered another hash mark in my book of local know-how.

When you are trying to find the eating spots that really click with you, it's like opening an unlabeled can and dining on the contents. You have no way to know that, while the house dressing is good enough to take intravenously, the marinara could be classified as a hazardous material. Or never go there any later than 6 p.m. because the noise level from the bar forces you to yell at the waitress like she just hacked your 401k and bought an alpaca farm with the proceeds.

So when a coworker recommended a great place for Italian food, we were grateful for the tip. Arriving at the address we found an ancient building, apparently dropped into the midst of an industrial campus by a sadistic tornado. There was an odor in the air that made me think that every junior high school boy in America had just opened his gym bag. We looked at each other.

"Sometimes these places have the best food," Bob offered with forced cheerfulness while I searched for evidence of a recent health department visit. I called the person who gave us the address and she responded with the comfortable laugh of a local. "Trust me, and get in there!" Three years later, it is still a favorite place of ours with wonderful food and a warm atmosphere.

Our epitome of dining newness happened on a Friday evening when I spotted a place that bragged about their proficiency with chicken wings. I am a native of Buffalo, New York, place of origin for that hallowed substance that really should be its own food group. The restaurant had a lot of people inside, always a good sign, but as we stepped through the door, the entire room went silent. I don't mean that a couple of folks glanced our way and continued eating. I mean everything stopped and all eyes set upon us like James Dean had just strolled into a girl's prep school. I pulled up short and felt my husband collide with my back. For a moment, nothing happened. I had a frozen smile on my face and a growing sensation that backpedaling out the door would be the better part of valor.

Suddenly, the blonde-haired lady behind the bar sang out, "Okay, people! It's just someone we don't know. Go back to what you're doing." They did and we crept forward. She seated us with a gracious smile, brought our beverages, and then got down to business. "So, what brings you to the Valley?"

We told her that I had taken a job here and Bob was coming to join me in a couple of months. She brightened and turned to him. "Well, honey, don't you worry about her. She'll be fine. If she wants to come have a drink, a lady can sit at the bar by herself with no trouble." My husband smiled his thanks and said, "Well, it's good

21

to know she won't get hit on." Our hostess frowned a bit and replied, "Oh, she'll get hit on, but they will be real sweet about it!" Off she went in search of menus, and Bob and I locked eyes in mutual wonder.

"Play our cards right and someday," I said, "we'll sail through the correct side of a three-way stop, remember not to order the marinara, and stare at people in the doorway."

"You want hot or nuclear?"

Wildlife

"Oh, look at the deer!"

Watching the animals from our hillside home was one of the best things about our rural relocation. In the beginning, it was so novel to us that all activity would stop while we watched in silent appreciation. I must have taken 500 pictures of deer that first year. I loved having close-up views of those sweet triangle faces and the bobby socks and Mary Janes coloring of their legs and hooves. Some of the newness has worn off, but we still enjoy our privileged "insider's view" of nature in her own.

There are days when I feel like the interloper, like I invaded their territory, which I guess is true. We have a consistent group of deer that enjoy the reclaimed field. There are many nights on the deck when our dinner companions are below, munching grass and turning an unconcerned eye to our perch once in awhile. There are turkey, raccoons and a beautiful red fox that treats us to hunting exhibitions on his visits.

All of which sounds idyllic, I know. But living in a rural area really can interfere with the demands of modern-day life. Heading out to work one morning, me in the lead with my husband behind, we encountered a large doe, defiantly standing in the path of both vehicles. I beeped the horn, I edged the car forward, but she simply glared at me. I was at a loss to understand her. A glance in the rearview mirror showed my husband, rocking his arms as though holding an infant. All became clear: she had a fawn nearby and did not like the look of us. As a parent myself, I looked at her with new empathy. She met my gaze calmly, as if to say, "I am protecting my own." We came to a compromise. I yielded the road to her and Baja'd the Jeep around the trees. (Compromise has a different definition out here.)

Sometimes the standoff is less subtle. Flying off the hill one day, already late, I encountered a veritable traffic jam of deer and turkey in the intersection. It looked like the opening session of a Rotary conference. ("Attention: If you are attending the lecture on 'Ten Ways To Get Past Garden Fences,', please head to the fourth tree on the right!") Feeling outnumbered, I leaned out the window and yelled, "I do not have time to star in a Disney movie today – move it!" Other times, we had to slow our vehicle as we followed a buck in rut trotting down the center of the road, nose to the pavement, reminding us that autumn is when a young male's fancy turns to love.

My significantly better half is normally a gentle soul with respect for all of God's creatures. Which is why I was surprised by the evil glint in his eye the day he said, "We have a woodchuck. A big one. He's got to go."

Bob had noticed the newly dug holes, a couple near the steps, a large one at the foundation. While I had no understanding what such dirt moving indicated, Bob was immediately on the alert. "He is shopping for a winter home. Well, he better start walking to Miami, because it isn't going to be with us!" Thus began "The Woodchuck War."

Luckily – or maybe not – our son was visiting from Texas and brought a concurring opinion with his dad that violence against the creature was warranted. I left the house with great trepidation that morning, fearing that I would return to our property looking like a missile test site with random holes dug everywhere. But the guys had a more surgical strike planned. They had found two ends of a tunnel and were plotting something akin to chasing down a runner between second and third base.

About halfway through my day, I received a photo via text from our daughter-in-law. Actually it was a sequence of two photos; the first showed our son inserting a billowing smoke bomb in one end of the gopher tunnel. The second depicted my husband, stationed on the lower deck, shotgun at the ready, intently watching the other end of said tunnel. A heartbeat later came the terse message from Sarah, "You might want to head home a little early."

Did you know that, if you *really* have to, you can U-turn on the Interstate?

I am relieved to report that all involved in the great woodchuck caper survived. Including the woodland creature, which I assume either watched with great amusement from a safe distance or owns a surplus WWII gas mask. I returned to faint clouds of pink still lingering over the field, the shotgun returned to storage and two amateur exterminators assessing the flaws in their plan over a couple of beers.

Whatever had happened, I had to smile a week or so later when I spotted his roly-poly gait lumbering down the hill. Though I am sure I imagined it, I would swear he forced himself awkwardly to a standing position, looked right at me and winked.

I neglected to tell my husband. Compromise has a different definition out here, you know.

The Baby Gets Married

"Will you marry me?"

As it was my assumption that Bob was down on the floor because he dropped his fork, the question caught me by surprise. They say you often don't recognize the most important moments in your life while they are happening. But I knew that decision would set me on a path unlike anything I had known. And I could not wait to tell my sisters.

When you are the baby of the family, there is a certain kind of joy that blesses your wedding day. You are the final line in the first chapter of your family book. I closed the door on the years when my parents and siblings resided together and it felt like each other was all we would ever need. I gave up the last holding on the family name and assumed a new one, along with a new family.

I think my sisters were bittersweet about their 30-something sibling finally tying the knot. Though it was hard to sort the smiles from the tears. Especially when they exclaimed to my only-child fiancé, "We would be happy it was anyone, but we are really happy it's you!"

Apparently, they had been harboring the fear that I would end up an old lady eating TV dinners in an unheated third-floor walk-up and lusting after Alex Trebek's moustache, without a husband.

So, with high hopes they awaited the details of the wedding. I found a dress I loved at a bridal shop in Elmira that promptly went out of business before our first anniversary. My sister suggested that once I was hitched, they figured that was the end of the single market and it was time to fold their tents. Bob was our city Fire Chief and he, and his groomsmen, were wearing their dress uniforms. We were forgoing many of the bridal traditions that we didn't like. No head table and formal introduction, no garter or bouquet toss, no force-feeding cake to each other. This was not Gidget marries Moondoggie. We were very grown-up people.

Two days before doing the "I do's", Terri, exercising her right as eldest sister, asked if Bob had reserved a limo for the ride to the reception. "No, we're just using the truck." The mortification on my sister's face could have dropped a crow out of the sky. "The truck" was a Dodge Ram, faded blue with cloth seats that had a stain from every condiment known to man and a few others we were still awaiting DNA results on.

"Robert! You are not taking my sister – in her wedding gown – in that...thing!"

"It's all washed and waxed and ready to go!"

I stayed out of it. My sisters and my future husband were going to have to work out their own relationship, and I knew to keep my head down until the ride came to a complete stop. Besides, I still couldn't believe this guy wanted to marry *me*. If he had suggested exchanging rocks in the forest and riding off on a tandem bike, I would have been in.

The day itself was a dream. The dress would have made Peppermint Patty look elegant, and I could see the love shining in Robert, so handsome and proud at the altar.

Everything went smoothly -- until it was time to light the unity candle. Bob's parents and my nieces had lit the two family candles. But when we tried to share those two flames into one, there was nothing but sizzling and crackling. No flame. We tried again, raising our eyes slightly to each other in a silent moment of growing panic. Snap, crackle, pop. The half dozen firefighters in the church, guys you can always count on to do what everyone else is thinking, began to snicker.

Finally, Father Mark could stand it no longer and leaned in with a classic stage whisper: "Turn them around. You have the wrong end!"

The congregation roared.

Correct ends applied and the new, combined candle for Maggie and Robert burst into color and warmth. Bobby gave me an apologetic shrug and said, "I can put them out. I can't start them." I laughed out loud.

I was breathless with joy. I wanted to dance with him right at that moment and get the "happily ever after" thing going. I savored the ending of the service when we were declared husband and wife.

In the video of the receiving line, you can now see something that was not evident to me on that magic day. While greeting our guests, Robert spent much time looking at two things: the train on my dress and his watch.

Upon leaving the church in a hail of rice and well wishes, our chariot was at the curb. Gleaming as Robert promised my sister. The passenger door was open, a white cloth was across the seat and a uniformed firefighter waited to help me into the cab of a 1997 American LaFrance fire engine. Terri, her mouth unhinged, stared at the fire truck and then slugged her new brother-in-law in the shoulder. "You rat!" It was the beginning of a beautiful friendship.

Yes, the country club hosting our reception did start to evacuate when we pulled up, and yes, we did need to apologize to the mayor for boosting one of his fire trucks, but it all worked out. We danced and sang and drank champagne and, as midnight transformed today into yesterday, we rode that faded Dodge Ram into our future.

Every love story is different. Not all of them include fire trucks and stubborn unity candles. Who cares if the person of your dreams shows up in a uniform, a flannel shirt or a business suit? Just so long as you hang on tight. And if you need a wedding-day vehicle, we have a used Dodge Ram for sale.

First Christmas on the Hill

"I know exactly where the Christmas tree will go."

It is an odd sentence to choke out in a whispered sob. But that is exactly how I said it, four years ago, upon walking into the living room of the next house for sale we were investigating.

A change in jobs required a move to the region overlapping northern Pennsylvania and southern New York. Husband Bob and I were on the second day of a two-day blur of available homes. In the golden light of an August afternoon, we were being driven up a steep hill while the real estate agent issued a string of disclaimers.

"I hesitate to show you this house. It's a bit....different."

The pause between "bit" and "different" was wide enough to sling a herd of cows through and Bob's worried glance caught mine in the side view mirror of the SUV. When pushed, the agent ticked off an itemized list of the challenges that awaited us.

"It's an older house, kind of a throw-back style. It's on a dirt road that is private, no municipal services and there are only three other homes. It hasn't been lived in for a while and –" he paused and dropped the vehicle into an even lower gear as the homes and businesses gave way to state land and forest.

"It's a little out of the way."

When we dropped down from the road onto a banked gravel drive, the house was about as impressive as Miley Cyrus' credentials to join the DAR. One story, overgrown field, no access from the road other than the driveway, which abruptly stopped at the door with no other option for exit besides backing up.

I entered while Bob tried to get a bit of perspective on the degree of slant the house was built into. When he joined me a few moments later, he wrinkled his forehead at the sight of me stopped in the entrance to the living room as though nailed to the floorboards. Instead of looking forward, he turned his concern to me. Tears were threatening to spill at any second and I looked out of breath. Before Bob could question I turned to him and uttered the sentence you read at the top.

Then Bob turned his head. The entire front of the house was glass. Floor to ceiling windows showcased a view of green-carpeted hills, cascading forward to a sky painted the blue from a child's storybook. Hardwood floors, a brick fireplace that offered a buffer between living and dining areas and a descending staircase filled his gaze. Snapped out of his trance by my holiday prophecy, he raised his hand and indicated the exact spot on the floor where a glistening evergreen stood in my mind's eye.

Fast forward to a brisk autumn morning as we rolled down the interstate, congratulating each other on the brilliance of our plan. No more stomping our feet on the frozen parking lot of a local business, as we had for countless Decembers. We were going to cut down our tree for the upcoming Christmas, but schlepping through the snow comparing spruces was for amateurs. We were going in the fall, tagging der Tannenbaum of choice in dry conditions and coming back in December for a fast cut and drag that would be surgical in its precision. As we got out of the truck, I asked my beloved if we had a tape measure handy. His response is one of the entries in the "Great Book of Phrases Uttered by Husbands That Give Wives the Heebee-Jeebees."

"Nope. I know how high the ceiling is."

This statement, when coupled with our mutual desire to attain "one honking big Christmas tree," should have been an indicator of what lie ahead. (On a related note, I am sure the Captain of the Titanic slapped his First Mate heartily on the back and said, "That iceberg don't look big, son! In fact, cut close to it and we will use the shavings to make margaritas tomorrow. Good night!")

Selection of our tree was a true team effort. I would attempt to gauge its shape and fullness. Bob would stand beside it, calculating its height by raising his arm over his head and doing the math based on his personal stats. Through this highly scientific method, we tagged a beauty estimated in the neighborhood of 12 feet tall. Perfect.

On the appointed day, deep into the holiday season, we returned, chopped the tree down and dragged it between us to the truck. We decided to forego the shaking and binding that the tree farm offered. To be honest, neither of us can recall now why we did that. (I think it's the residual shock suppressing our memories, but I digress.) The tree snuggled comfortably inside the eight-foot bed, with a dainty section of about a foot jutting over the tailgate.

"Drat! We miscalculated! It can't be but nine feet tall!" I jammed my gloved hands into my jacket pockets and turned to Bob with a scowl. "That's going to look pretty stumpy in our front room."

Bob was quiet, the usual sign that his brain is analyzing the situation the way a MRI dissects a scan, layer-by-layer and angle-by-angle.

"It's just fallen deeper into the truck bed than I thought it would. It's still at least ten feet tall and, either way, it's ours now. Let's go."

At home, we propped open the front door, dropped the tailgate of the truck and hauled that evergreen into the middle of the living room floor. And that's when it happened - the moment our kids refer to as the "Magic Morphing Christmas Tree of 2011." I prefer to remember it as the moment I turned to my husband and demanded, "Just how short do you think you are?"

The beast, for that is surely what it had become, obscured the living room floor for a solid five feet from side-to-side and a mind-blowing

15 feet from bottom to tip. It was an endless mass of forest green boughs. I swear to you I heard it growl. One of our cats had ventured out to investigate and when the tree did its "Creature from the Black Lagoon" impersonation, she dropped her ears flat, hissed like a busted boiler and shot back down the stairs.

I wanted to go with her.

"Babe? Did somebody swap trees on us?"

Bob rolled his eyes and said, "Yep, that's it Mags. There is a band of tree swappers who must have hung off an overpass on I-86 and grabbed our tree and replaced it with this Sequoia. Call CSI: Kings' Canyon."

When are husbands going to learn that sarcasm in the face of sincerity is akin to reaching for the lemon juice after a paper cut? Ultimately painful and oh so preventable.

Our usual tree stand looked like something from the Barbie Playhouse when we tried to jam it on the stump of the trunk. I could see the blue-eyed MRI cranking up again and a trip to the garage produced a large bucket, a couple of bricks and a sack of sand, all remnants from the extensive remodeling we had done.

The tree was nearly impossible to subdue and the fact that it smelled like every good childhood memory you ever had did not negate the fact that it was stabbing me a hundred times a minute. On the count of three, the tree went up, up, up and into the bucket and down. The down was not nearly as impressive as the up and, to my horror, the evergreen from Hell bent at least two feet of its crowning points against the newly painted ceiling. Had it been metal-on-metal it would have made your teeth hurt to listen to. The needles cut a delicate pattern into the beige paint and came to rest at a cockeyed angle, causing the entire tree to list 15 degrees to port.

The rest of the day is a blur. It took us four hours, two additional stump trimmings, three bags of sand and enough high-gauge fishing line to hog tie a Sumo wrestler to secure the tree. The two of us fell onto the sofa in an exhausted pile, silently surveying the wreckage. Chunks of hacked off boughs and trunk littered the floor along with yards of fishing line and bailing twine. About a half gallon of water had sloshed out of the bucket at one point, bringing with it enough wet sand to nest a family of pelicans. A paltry box of ornaments, more than adequate for all of our past trees, looked as if it would, maybe, cover the top third. If we put a string of lights on every available bough, confused pilots would overshoot the Elmira-Corning airport and try to land DC-9s on our deck.

"You know," Bob gasped between gulps of air, "I think the natural look is the best for this Christmas. Less showy decorations. Maybe just a few ornaments and some pine cones. What do you think?"

I nodded, being unable to form words. My lungs had crawled out my mouth to see what the heck was going on. My face felt perforated, like someone was going to tear it off a college bulletin board advertising for roommates.

When I could, I squeaked, "Is this a Scotch Pine?" Bob rocked his head no.I was crestfallen.

"I was hoping that would be justification for a glass of Dewar's."

The MRI had enough juice left for one more calculation.

"Actually, Honey, it's a rare species. A 'Bourbonite'. Yep. And I believe tradition dictates a glass of Maker's Mark for toasting it."

He may think he is only four feet tall, but I still love the way his mind works.

The Wild Side of the Hill

"David, let me call you back. We have company."

It was Super Bowl Sunday, the highest of holy days for football fans, and I was ensconced in the recliner in our family room. Adult beverage on one side table, wonderfully unhealthy fried food on the other and me, wrapped in total bliss, in the deep center of the chair. A slate gray day blew at the porch windows in the late afternoon gloom. The fireplace danced orange light around the room while my husband chatted on the phone with our youngest.

I had been in heavy contemplation over the unlikelihood of Seattle having any hope of shutting down Tom Brady, when Bob's sign-off on the phone call snapped me back to the moment. Company? I hadn't heard the doorbell or the distinctive sound of tires chewing on the gravel in our sloped driveway.

"We have visitors? Who's here?"

Bob, a man you could not rattle if you hit him with a tire iron, pointed to a spot on the far side of the carpet and calmly said, "Snake."

In my humble opinion, nothing surrounding the existence of snakes should ever be approached calmly. I am an ardent proponent of screaming, flailing of arms, excessive cursing, and pleas to the Almighty for intervention. And speed. All of this must be conducted in a blur of color, indistinguishable to the human eye. Height is good, too, meaning elevation of any sort, by any means. I once hovered above the ground for a solid two minutes while my hiking partner dispatched a reptile. Think it can't be done? Watch me.

In this particular instance, I had gone from my backside to my feet in one motion and in the next moment was standing, balanced on the now oscillating recliner. (I've tripped over lint on the floor, but when a snake is introduced into the picture, I am a flippin' Wallenda.) From this position, I had a clear view of the snake.

It – no, I didn't know the gender and you can bet your anti-venom kit I was not about to find out – was lying on the artificial turf of our carpet. To my eyes, it was nine feet long, as big around as municipal drainage pipe, with fangs that looked like Dracula's dentist had branched into veterinary work. Bob stood a scant couple of feet away from it and lazily questioned, "Now, how did he get in here?"

How? Who cares how? If you encounter a homicidal maniac twirling an axe you don't waste time wondering which exit off of I-86 he took to get here! Just do something to remove yourself from the situation!

Bob knew without looking that I was doing my high-wire act on the La-Z-Boy. He moved to the linen closet and returned with a large bath towel. He peered closer at the creature and smiled. "Mags, look how pretty he is."

I had yet to breathe and when I inhaled it sounded like a choking vacuum cleaner.

"Get it out of here."

Bob removed the snake without incident. It was another in the seemingly endless encounters we have with the creatures that called this hill home long before we got here.
Some of the episodes are gentle and mutually beneficial, like watching from inside while the deer graze or the birds practice landings on the feeder platform like pilots returning to the aircraft carrier.

Other times, though, the introduction of a critter into our world is a bit more intrusive.

Thanksgiving night, some of our family braved the cold, the crowds and the cynicism of "Black Thursday" shopping. It was near midnight when our daughter Angie, family friend Brent and I returned home and began assembling turkey sandwiches (which are the whole reason behind Thanksgiving, can I get an Amen?) Brent announced that one of the cats had cornered a mouse in the kitchen.

Said cat toted said mouse right down the hallway, intent on presenting her find to her favorite human, my husband. He, having no appetite for crazed shopping sprees, was already asleep. Brent gave chase, but the mouse had escaped into the closet in the bedroom.

So – at approximately midnight on Thanksgiving night - I nudged my better half awake with the news that there was a mouse on the rampage in the room. By the way, I added, your daughter is also here, so don't go flinging those covers off unless you want to foot the bill for extensive therapy in the years to come. It is a credit to Robert's ability to adapt and overcome that he said nothing and merely rolled over.

A chase ensued that involved both of the young people, both cats and the frantic mouse. At one point, the rodent sought refuge under a dresser and Brent dropped to his knees before it. I assumed he was triangulating a path of escape when the mouse, for reasons that remain unknown to this day, rocketed out from the dresser and directly into Brent's…uh….nether regions.

I now present the second case study that a human being can take flight when properly motivated. Well done, Brent.

The images that follow are a bit graphic for a family publication, so let's leave it with the crowd of us trooping back out of the room with

Brent carrying the unconscious creature and a firm conviction to wear an athletic cup when dining late with the Barneses.

All of which brings us to the bear.

Many of the residents of our hill had spoken of seeing a large bear roam the woods. He had been found grocery shopping in some of the finer garage refrigerators and, in one memorable visit, decimated a 50-count box of pudding cups. But he hadn't been near enough to us to be sighted. Then Scott, resident of the last house on our tiny four-house road, brought down video from the night before. The birdfeeder on their deck stands seven feet tall and the bear was snacking from it like he was leaning on a table in the bar waiting for the hostess to seat his party. Scott had whispered to his wife Peggy, "I'm gonna open the slider so I can get better video of him." To which Peggy replied, "No, you're not, because I look lousy in black."

Bob pouted. "Everyone has seen the bear but us!" I, on the other hand, planned to live a long, fabulously fulfilled life minus any bear visits.

So, a week later, while working on our home office, I truly had no idea what I was hearing outside. The bottom half of our house is built into a hillside, so the side windows are at ground level. I had to put both hands to the glass to bring the picture into view.

The thought formed, "Why am I looking at the bottom of the recycling bin?"

Because the bear had tipped it over.

He was 450 pounds if he was an ounce, with a head the size of a hubcap and black as night. I have to say, I was impressed with my own composure. I walked into the family room and simply said, "Robert. You asked about the bear? He's here."

We watched the woodland creature sit upright and, with surprising gentleness, pull each of the bags out of the bin and slice them open. He must have thought he had found a candy store when he came on the tray liner from our recent painting. He was probably anticipating more of that sweet pudding, but when he lifted the liner, he was not impressed with the beige paint that dripped down his nose. He tried to catch some of it on his tongue until his taste buds kicked in. The tray was noisily discarded, and I was sure our Trip Advisor rating had just been downgraded.

But the next discovery was the bucket of fried chicken remnants and our four-star dining status was restored.

After a brief stay at the toppled bin, he rolled to his feet and ambled up the driveway. I'm sure he saw us at the window and I'm equally confident that he knew there was nothing to fear.

If he talked to the local snakes at all, he knew I was a non-issue.

I was ready to check off another on the list of our country adventures and Bob was beaming. Then a cloud passed over his face. "What's the matter?" I asked.

"He didn't stay long. We need to throw out a better grade of garbage."

Somebody hand me a tire iron.

Working Like a Dog

"Are you sure about this?"

I locked eyes with Bob, conscious of the weight of this decision and wanting to be as confident as I could be about his feelings.

"We've talked about this for years," my husband said. "It's now or never."

"We're pretty old to be adding a little one to the family."

"All the more reason to do it now while we still have some energy."

I looked again at the image on the computer screen and felt my heart swell.

"He is beautiful," I conceded.

So after a lot of preparation, four weeks later, a smiling man laid in my arms a squirming 12-week old puppy.

Rex is a rescue dog, so his lineage is a bit cloudy. We know there is some German shepherd, but Daddy didn't stick around for a paternity test, the scoundrel. So, we can guess at Border collie, retriever of some flavor or a splash of Beagle, but the fact is we don't know. Nor do we care. Rex is a bundle of energy, slobbery kisses and a classic "what's-that-sound" head tilt that stole our hearts from day one.

Having a dog for the first time in our long marriage has presented us with some logistical challenges. Bob's retirement was a key factor in getting Rex, as we felt strongly that working full-time would not give us the kind of opportunities we needed to invest in raising a young dog. That's worked out fine. Except this one time…

Our daughter-in-law had earned her doctorate, a glorious achievement that she managed to pull off while being married to an Air Force officer and giving birth to the world's cutest grandson. (Stand down the counter claims – we aren't opening that can of worms.) Bob and daughter Angie decided to make a whirlwind drive to North Carolina, attend the graduation ceremony and then blast back up the coast by Sunday night.

That plan left me a solo puppy parent on a workday, so I let my fingers do the clicking and found a certified dog sitter not far from my office. She had good reviews and repeat clients, so I felt certain she could handle one lively shepherd-and- whatever-else-he-is.

In the dark hours of Friday morning, I sent my family off on their trip and a couple of hours later, loaded Rex into the car with enough cargo to support an entire colony of puppies. Food, treats, six toys, his bed, favorite blanket, medical record, both leashes, a spare collar and a quantity of poop bags a Bull Mastiff would be embarrassed about.

The sitter's house was small, but neat and I said lots of reassuring things to Rex as I carried him up the steps. "This will be fun! She even has a dog, so you will make a new friend. You'll spend all day playing! This is great!"

I rang the doorbell and the stillness of the morning was shattered by a cacophony of noise from the other side of the door. A crash, barking, some yelling, more barking, another crash, the sound of canine nails digging into woodwork, more barking. Rex's ears went flat and when the door was yanked open, revealing a young woman straining to hold back a massive dog, Rex began to tremble in my arms.

She coaxed us inside, using both hands on a short leash to restrain her dog. Pretty animal, and its
tail thumped wildly, but the way he lunged and pulled at us was starting to panic both Rex and me. We sat on sofas in the tiny living room. The resident dog twisted and jumped and tried every evasive maneuver taught at Top Gun to get away from its owner.

"He calms down after awhile!" The young woman smiled as she shouted over the din.

I sat there, my 4 month-old baby trying to bore a hole in my chest to hide in, and thought about all the "must-dos" on my desk at work.

"Isn't he used to bigger dogs?" She called out.

I look at the dog sitter and fought hard not to say, "Yes, he is. But not Cujo."

In the end, I just could not do it. I knew, if I left Rex in that house, I would be in a state of near panic all day. It was no good. I had no choice. We drove to my office and I walked Rex on the grass that frames the parking lot.

"Okay Rex, listen up," I lectured as we walked. "We have to go into the office for a little while. I'll get some work off my computer and we will go home. Please be a good boy."

He didn't like the elevator ride, but the fuss my incredible boss and coworkers made over him put the sparkle back into his face.

"We'll close him up in our section," my officemate Carol suggested. "He'll be fine."

That's what we did and I was frantically printing, emailing and piling papers in my office when I looked out the door toward the waiting room. Rex was in the center of the space, head tilted, eyes closed and an expression of pure contentment on his face while he deposited an exact replica of Mt. Rainier on the carpet. We're talking a Dairy Queen double-scoop, swirled perfectly right to the little fold-over at the top. A heartbeat later, the smell exploded in the air.

"Carol!" I managed to gasp.

"Now, that's impressive," she exclaimed. "That's gotta be half his body weight."

Professional humiliation comes in many forms. Maybe you botched the big sales presentation. Maybe you were introducing your boss at a conference and went blank when you got to his name. Did you write an email to your friend in which you described a coworker as being "dumb as a sack of hair", and then accidently send it to the sack in question?

Those are nothing compared to being on your knees with a bottle of disinfectant, trying to lift a stain the shape of Africa out of the carpet while your coworkers attempt to corral your dog. It took three poop bags, many paper towels and intervention by the professionals in Housekeeping to render the office habitable again.

Back in the car, Rex put his front paws on the center console and gave me a doggie grin that said, "What a great day! What are we gonna do next, Mom?"

I shrugged at him and smiled back.

"I don't know, Rex. How are you at writing resumes?"

A Different Drive-Thru

"Welcome to Dunkin' Donuts. What can I get you?"

I shoved the Jeep into park, the excessive use of force a proper
indicator of my lousy mood. I was hot. I was tired. I was frustrated
with the state of humankind in general.

Six months into a new job and I was still struggling to understand the
processes essential to my position. Earlier that day, I had a hefty
portion of my backside handed to me by an unhappy client. I pride
myself on my professional abilities and every error and misjudgment
was carried home and brooded upon. My boss, a most supportive
and congenial chap, tried to settle my knotted nerves. "You'll get it,"
he smiled. "You're still learning." He had more patience than I did
for a ramp-up I found inexcusably long.

There was more eating at me than the job. As spring had come to a
close, my family suffered the loss of a brother and, though the death
had been expected, grief continued to hang over my heart like a
morning fog that wouldn't lift.

My tolerance for the small infractions of social behavior that make
up modern life had bottomed out. Every slow driver, disinterested
store clerk and ill-tempered mechanical device unleashed a reaction

from me that was out of proportion. I would have slugged Gandhi if he tried to get through the express lane with 11 items.

I was grouchy.

I contemplated telling the chipper voice on the speaker that she could get me a new mindset and a return to a generous nature, but I doubted they had that among the blueberry bagels and Boston crèmes. I ordered a strawberry smoothie and dutifully pulled ahead when advised.

There were two cars in front of me, one at the window having some sort of conversation with the cashier.

"Oh, come on," I grumbled, "no chatting today. Just give me my damn smoothie."

The first car pulled away and the one in front of me took its place. Again, there was much gesturing and back-and-forth between the car and the person inside the window.

"If they are doing a customer survey or something, I will pull her through that window and stuff her in the glove box," I sneered.

Like I said – grouchy.

After what seemed like enough time to negotiate the purchase of the entire franchise, the car before me moved on. I rolled into place, debit card in hand and a face of granite. Ain't making nice with nobody today.

Then I looked at the young lady gazing at me from the other side of the split windows. She couldn't have been 20 years old, vibrant swath of pink hair in her ponytail. But the dye job had nothing on the brightness of her eyes. They were shining. In fact…was she about to cry? Oh, what the hell…

"Okay," she gasped out, struggling to contain her emotions. "I don't know what to say…the people in front of you," she gestured to the minivan negotiating a left-hand turn out of the lot, "they paid for your order."

That stopped me dead in my miserable, self-absorbed tracks.

But she had more.

"And the people in front of them paid for them and the people in front of them paid for them and…it's been going on for half an hour! I just don't even know…"

She stopped talking, back of her hand to her mouth and the battle against the tears being lost.

The whole idea of this kind of random generosity tried to settle into my blackened brain, but failed. It certainly didn't jive with my current worldview. It was like watching a black and white movie, but one person keeps showing up in full color. This doesn't make sense, not today. I was in a full-blown, grade A, diva snit!

I looked again at my benefactors, driving off in a nondescript, dirty, soccer mom van with a dented bumper. The concept of such a sweet act tried to crawl into my brain again, and failed again. 'People do not do things like this. Not in this day and age,' I mused. And yet there she was, all nineteen years of her, breathing around her tears and beaming at me with pure joy. I felt like Ebenezer scowling into the face of Tiny Tim.

I had to close my eyes when the afternoon sun cleared a cloud and flooded my windshield with light. When the reality of the moment planted a flag in my head, successfully this time, it wasn't because the reality had turned right side up. It was because my head had.

My debit card was still in my fingers, and a glance in the rearview mirror told me all I needed to know for the next few moments of my life.

"Then I'm paying for them," I jerked my head behind me.

"Oh!" She took a step back from the window and put her hand to the top of her head. "There's three people in that car!"

"Good," I snapped with something that could have sounded like irritation. "I hope they're hungry."

She processed my card and looked at the receipt.

"Honestly, I've never seen anything like this. I don't know what's gotten into everyone today," she said, shaking her head.

She went on. "I mean, you just paid $13.63 for one smoothie!"

I took the offered cup and receipt and pondered the number at the bottom of the tally.

$13.63? To buy back my soul?

What a bargain.

Trouble in Texas

"We have to get to C-17!"

I searched the cavernous innards of O'Hare International Airport for a gate number and came up with C-2. Oh, my achin' head.

The flight from Elmira had been grounded by fog so thick you could have written your name in it. Now we were racing to our connecting flight. It was a Friday in August and every man, woman, child and tiny dog in America had tracked our online reservations and decided, "Let's go, too!" It was a madhouse.

The situation at our intended gate was the worst scenario possible. The plane was still nestled against the jet-way, tantalizingly near the window we peered out from. But the aircraft door was closed and, as the beleaguered agent explained to our panting faces, "Once that door is closed, the plane is gone." Robert's logical mind rebels against regulatory restrictions that run counter to reality. "But, it's right *there*!" he argued, to no avail.

We were as cranky as an old lady whose lucky bingo cards got snatched up. Especially when they were taken by that new woman, the one who always wears eyeshadow that matches her shoes, and who does she think she is kidding with that hair? It hasn't been that color since the first Reagan Administration.

Anyway, the rebooking of our tickets on a later flight resulted in two boarding passes in the name of Robert Barnes. So we set the alarm off at the gate. Further complicating the situation was the fact that Robert was already on the plane. Yep, another man with my husband's exact name happened to be on the same flight. For just a moment, I fondly thought of a past beau with the last name Vallelunga. Go ahead, Delta, try to find another one of those on your plane! Ha!

Anyway, we touched down in Texas nine sweaty hours after we left the breezes of our Waverly home. As we stood in line for our rental car, I reminded myself why we were doing this.

Few people travel to Houston in August without extradition papers and an escort from the U.S. Marshalls, but our first grandchild was being formally welcomed into the family of God. Nothing was keeping us from her christening, not even the need for oven mitts on the steering wheel of our rental. We hit another hiccup when we got to the security gate at the car center. "I'm sorry," the attendant said, "but Robert is not listed as the primary driver. It has to be the person who paid for the reservation." Note to self: get Bobby's name on the darn AmEx. So we bailed out of the car right at the gate and scrambled ourselves into the approved positions. I got us off airport property, but the specter of Friday afternoon traffic in Houston loomed, and we reversed the seating back at the first wide spot in the road I could find.

We brought our GPS, but it seemed to be suffering from mechanical heatstroke.

"Do you recognize that shopping plaza?" On one of our forays, I pointed and Bob shrugged. "This place is nothing but shopping plazas. They all look alike." Trying to make ourselves useful, we had offered to pick up the food for the after-baptism gathering. "When you make that turn, Costco will on the left." Yes, it was - on the left hand side of a six-lane highway, on which we were traveling in the opposite direction. "Turning left," meant getting off at the next exit, turning left under the overpass and getting back on the left side, which is now the right side.

Frustration mounting, Bob and I admitted to each other that what city driving skills we possessed had been whitewashed clean in five years of living in a place that defines "traffic" as the ability to see another car on the same road. Might be two cars a mile off but, "Look at the traffic today!"

And the heat. Houston in August is brutally hot and humid, a feeling that permeates your every pore. I never seemed to get dry and my eyeballs were swimming in circles, producing a headache I could have put out to bid to major pharmaceutical companies. As Bob quipped, "I prefer to live somewhere I can shovel my way out of my problems."

During the ceremony, Annabelle wailed appropriately, thinking her parents had lost their minds in handing her over to a robed stranger who was trying to drown her. We beamed.

The night before our departure, we schemed to swing back to the house early on Monday and snatch up David and Kristina, son #2 and his wife, as their flight was leaving within minutes of ours. The purpose was to avoid dragging son #1 back out of the house needlessly for a long drive into the city.

In the predawn light, I kissed the chubby cheeks of the still-drowsy Annabelle and whispered, "Grandma and Grandpa love you very much. But we are never coming to see you in August again!"

We were 15 minutes into an expected hour and a half ride when David's voice popped over the backseat and into my ear. "You guys are flying out of Hobby, right?"

"The airport. The one we always fly into."

"Let me see your ticket."

Wherever you are right now, point to the farthest spot in the room on your left. That's Bush Intercontinental Airport, from which Robert and I were flying. Now, turn and point to the right, as far away as you can get. That's Hobby Airport, where the kids needed to be.

Sigh.

Several options were considered and discarded to deal with this travel tragedy. We ended up summoning son #1 out of his home anyway, to retrieve his brother and sister-in-law and take them, at a high rate of fuel consumption, to the correct airport.

As we watched our kids walk back down the ramp of the parking garage, their rolling luggage flashing behind them in the Texas heat, my heart sank. They would have to cover a good chunk of ground on foot to get to a corner where Eric could reach them. I turned to find my husband's face just as pained as mine.

"There goes 'Parents of the Year'." I said. "Right down the crapper."

Everyone made it where they needed to be and I really don't want to know how. Nothing made the local news, so I'm happy.

A day later I was unwinding the garden hose from the side of the house, calculating how much I would need to reach the flower box on the lower deck. The large oak outside the dining room had been pelting us with acorns all summer. Quiet evenings were punctuated by the BONG of tiny brown missiles ricocheting off the stainless steel grill. I stepped on to the side hill and it was like trying to walk on ball bearings. A carpet of acorns grabbed my feet, rolled me ten feet straight down like a high-speed assembly line and plopped me on my butt for the final few feet. My hands had constricted in a failed attempt to hold on to something, resulting in the hose nozzle locking in the "on" position. I slid to a dusty, muddy stop with the garden hose spewing water like a crazed snake and acorns crammed into parts of my body that should have required a formal introduction.

I laid there and had one thought.

"It's good to be home."

Who Is That?

"How many people live here?"

Life in a small town is different on many levels. The pace is slower and, I think, more practical. You may have fewer acquaintances, but relationships tend to be deeper. There's a simple reason for that. Get a town small enough and there isn't much else to watch except each other.

I was once in a quaint burg whose town clerk had a sign on the wall that said, "We don't need directionals on our cars here. Everyone knows where you are going."

For a recent holiday, Bob and I received a lovely set of cordial glasses, beautifully etched and delicate. When we were unloading gifts from the car that night, we demonstrated perfect miscommunication when it came to handling that box.

"Got it?"
"Got it."
CRASH!
"Oh, that? No, I didn't have that."

Only one of the glasses cracked, but I was heartsick. The next business day I hurried to the store the box had come from and crossed my fingers for a bit of luck. Staring into the display cabinet of a dozen varieties of glasses, I had a sudden mental block about which were the ones we had been given. When the clerk offered to assist me, I lamented that we broke a glass that had been a gift and I couldn't remember the pattern. Without a word, she opened the case, plucked the exact crystal I needed and held it out to me. "This one, Mrs. Barnes," she smiled.

That's what happens when a store can remember who bought what for whom.

All of this was brought to mind on a chilly spring evening when we were attending to sad duty; calling hours for an elderly friend who had passed. He had lived his entire life in a hamlet of less than a thousand people and it looked like most of them had turned out to say farewell. The line went out the door of the funeral home and a good distance down the sidewalk.

While we waited, everyone chatted. We talked about the weather, how the winter had been, gas prices, what crops were going in the ground as soon as Mother Nature settled on which season it was going to be.

The conversation suddenly hushed as someone who had been inside made his way past the line and back out to the parking lot. A middle-aged man, sporting a dark beard and mustache, nodded politely to those in line and stepped out into the twilight.

Then it started. In the next 94 seconds, the crowd pooled its collective memory.

"Who was that?"

"Anyone recognize him?"

"Is he a Martin? He looked like one of the Martin kids."

"With a beard? Tsk! Sarah wouldn't have allowed it!"

"Is he the guy who bought the hardware store?"

"No, that guy is taller. And he'd wear flannel, even to a funeral."

"I think I saw him at the Post Office on Saturday."

"You didn't even go to the Post Office on Saturday. I went. And I didn't see him!"

"He's getting on a motorcycle!"

"Well then, see? Clearly, he isn't a Martin."

"I have no idea. This is so strange."

My neck hurt from swiveling in so many directions, trying to keep up with the flow of speculation and historical knowledge. The group then settled into quiet, puzzling, as Dr. Seuss would say, "Until their puzzlers were sore."

I took a deep breath and in my best educational tone said, "You know, it is possible that Don, somewhere in the course of his long, productive life, met someone who isn't from here."

I was met with a silence a mason could have constructed a fine wall out of. A thought had not been received with such skepticism since

Christopher Columbus had stood in the court of Queen Isabella and said, "Izzy, I am telling you. It's round as the King's fat head! Now, hand over the cash, I gotta catch a boat."

There is a fine line between small-town familiarity and a level of personal knowledge that begs for a restraining order. As the days of spring warmed the ground and the breeze sighed in relief from the cold, I got a call from our dry cleaner.

"Maggie, we have a dress of yours down here. Been here awhile," the voice on the phone said.

I was bewildered, almost certain I wasn't missing anything from my closet, but I swung in on my next drive through town. I was handed a polka-dotted summer frock that I knew on sight was, indeed, mine. Then I noticed that there was no name on the plastic bag. No receipt or order form – nothing.

"Matt," I said, accepting my change, "how did you know this dress was mine?"

With nary a trace of apology to his tone, he replied, "Oh, I remember seeing you in it last summer."

In a larger community, a comment like that would have registered a 9 on the creepy scale. In our little intersection of the world, it was perfectly understandable. I remembered the day I wore that dress last summer. There wasn't much else going on.

A Girl and Her Car

"The car is making a funny noise."

My husband will tell you that this is one of the most terrifying statements a wife can make to her spouse. According to him, it rates just above, "I ran into your old girlfriend today." And just below, "I'm leaving you and I'm not taking the children."

While the color had drained out of his face, I was serenely calm. Cars and I have always had a complicated relationship. I had owned quite a range. My first was a 1973 Dodge Charger with a V8 that would purr to me, "Wanna pass that truck? Relax, I've got this." It was baby poop green and one day gave birth to a herd of tiny squirrels in the parking lot of my college.

Many years later, while working for a non-profit organization, I pulled into the parking lot of a car dealership to pick up a donation. The owner and his father watched me turn the car off, then, as was its habit, the car sputtered and rocked and choked for several moments more. As it did, I skillfully crawled over the passenger seat and exited, the driver's door having long since rusted shut. (Considering I was in a dress at the time, I thought I was the very vision of grace.) Just as I reached the door, the car gave one last heave and threw up most of the contents of the radiator before falling silent.

Presenting myself to the owners, I was taken aback when the elder of the two turned to his son and said, "I'm not going to sleep tonight if she leaves in that car. Do something."

It started when I needed it to. It stopped somewhere in the vicinity of where it should have. What's the problem?

Crappy cars were just a way of life for me during my salad days, which consisted of lots of lettuce and not much else. You haven't experienced automotive trauma until your transmission decides to commit suicide on a hill during a snowstorm, rendering the letters on your shifter meaningless. I once had to sign a disclaimer before a repair shop would let me leave. I had gotten all the repairs I could afford, far fewer than the ones they recommended for, you know, "safe operation" and all that technical mumbo-jumbo.

So, it was a treat to have a nice car, sold to me by that horrified and sympathetic car dealer. I loved that car and drove it for years. And years. It was that car I presented to my husband with my concern about noise.

I told Bob my ride would squeak when the brakes were applied. He offered to listen for himself and I watched him pull away from the house. The first stop sign was not more than 50 feet down the street, so I watched as the car shuddered to a halt. For a moment, it just sat there. Bob just sat there. I was bewildered.

Then the back-up lights came on and the vehicle rolled in reverse at a much slower pace. Bob got out and I immediately noticed that the color had returned to his face. It was gray.

"How long has it been doing that?" He braced himself against the hood, as if the power had gone out of his legs.

I shrugged. "A month or so."

In a whirlwind matter of minutes, we were off to our neighborhood mechanic, but Bob insisted on driving my car with me following in his. Odd. Bob and Kenny had a brief conversation and the car expert promised a prompt look-see.

We hadn't been home ten minutes when Kenny called and requested that "both of you come back right now."

There sat my two-tone blue beauty, with the rear right tire removed. The car seemed to be balancing on a stack of concrete blocks, which I thought was the weirdest stand-in jack I ever saw.

Then I noticed that Kenny's face had the same dingy tinge that I had seen earlier. What is it with these guys…a bladder infection?

"Maggie," Kenny began in a strained voice. "I can't repair this car."

Before I could respond he brought me to the open rear hatch and pointed down.

"I wanted to put the back seat down to get a better look at the wheel wells. When I pulled the release tabs on your seat, the entire wheel fell off!"

Sure enough, the concrete blocks were doing what the tire used to; hold up the car. All around the blocks I could see clear to the floor of the garage.

"Okay." I said, before noticing that my husband had put his hand over his mouth. "So, fix it."

Kenny's mouth opened and closed a couple of times before his voice emerged. Or rather, the voice of a 10-year old girl who has just been invited to a sleepover at Taylor Swift's house.

"Fix it? I can't fix this! Henry Ford couldn't fix this!"

He dropped to his knees and rolled under the car, his face appearing in the gaping hole where the tire had been.

"Can you see me?"

"Sure!"

"You're not supposed to!"

Another technical conversation followed, something about the shock tower rusting right out of the thing and taking the wheel with it. I repeated my earlier shrug and offered a helpful suggestion.

"Just weld the tire back on."

Kenny was starting to look like that cartoon illustration of what a heart attack victim looks like. His eyes bulged; his chest billowed in and out. The man should really cut down on the caffeine.

"Weld it?" He bellowed. "Weld it to what? There's nothing there!" Again, I watched his grease stained hands frantically wave under the car.

The diagnosis was tough to take. This vehicle had never let me down. It started every single time. It had the soul of a warrior. It had character and courage. The body had simply worn out. Was it not human? If you pricked it, would it not bleed black 10-30? After a talk with Bob about the full life my blue beauty had had, I decided to donate the car to research. The guys from the auto shop class at the high school came with a flatbed. I cried.

Today, I tool around in a pretty SUV with a dashboard that looks like I could launch the missiles at NORAD from it. It glides along with power-this and auto-that. I'm cocooned in a cockpit of surround sound, side airbags and cruise control. My current mechanic has clean hands, a spotless uniform and a computer that tells him when my magic carpet has so much as a head cold.

What's the fun in that?

Stepping Carefully

"Do you have children?"

For the majority of the world this question is so easy to answer it is almost a reflex. For me, this query kicks off a fairly sophisticated calculation in my head. Who's asking? What is my relationship with the asker? How much of this do I want to get into?

Spies are trained to run this same brain path as a safeguard against revealing secret information. My position is only slightly less dangerous.

I'm a stepparent.

In the course of a lovely, one-hour ceremony in a small church I went from being a single gal with a cat to a wife with three kids, 6, 10 and 16 years old.

My best friend said, "I cannot imagine you as a Mom."

I replied, "I'm not going to be a Mom. They have a Mom. I'm going to be an ancillary adult with no discernible purpose. I'm the appendix of parenting. But more charming."

It was like starting a book on page 224. I didn't know any of the characters, I barely knew the setting and I sure didn't know the plot. "Can I go to Pat's house today?"

How would I know? Are Pat's parents Ward and June Cleaver? Or people with a chainsaw collection and pets that keep disappearing? Will you end up stealing hubcaps if I let you go? What if they trigger your allergies? Do you have allergies?

I spent the entire first year of my marriage saying, "Ask your father."

The first holiday season after our wedding, Robert decided I should spend a day alone with the kids to bond with them. As the teenager, Eric was convinced he needed another parent like a pig needs eye shadow and opted out. We had a couple of false starts, like when the jelly I gave them for their toast had a touch of mold in it. I tried to tell them it was a hedge against strep. No sale.

Angela and David and I had a good time wandering the mall, ending with chicken fingers and ice cream. But my rising heart nosedived when David announced that he needed to use the restroom. All six years of him was adamant that he could use the men's room unescorted. I was petrified. Is there a firm age on these things? Had the Internet been invented, I would have been Googling the hell out of the issue.

I instructed David to go in, do his thing and come right back out. Do not speak to anyone. Do not make eye contact with anyone. If you need me, call me. I said this with the earnestness born of fear. He nodded solemnly and headed in. I stood in front of the bathroom door, glaring at every man in the restaurant, daring them to give in to their bladders. Not on my watch. After a few minutes of quiet, my calm exterior was shattered by a desperate cry.

"*Maggie!*"

I had never before felt the combination of panic and adrenaline that flooded my system. I all but took the bathroom door off the hinges, charging into the small space with murderous intent. I was prepared to confront the gang of kidnappers that everyone knows hangs out in mall restrooms. Instead, I found David, standing at the sink, rocking up on his toes to reach the faucet. He was waving his hands under the motion-activated water, the delight evident on his face.

"Look! I don't have to turn the water on and it comes on!"

As fast as the surge of energy poured through me, it drained out and I slumped against the door, barely able to stand. The red haze cleared my eyes and I managed a smile.

"That's great, D. Just…great."

There were many more moments of varying shades of panic in the ensuing years. There was yelling and tears and anger and sweet laughter and times of near perfect family love. I stumbled my way through, complete with lots of wrong decisions and bucket loads of self-doubt. In many ways, the kids and I grew up together.

I became someone I couldn't even have envisioned for myself. Did I really make a blanket fort out of the living room furniture and crunch my spine lying on the floor to watch a Disney movie? Was that me, yelling myself hoarse and clapping frozen hands on soccer sidelines? Who was that woman, staring at the ceiling at midnight until I heard a key in the door and the reassuring sound of the refrigerator swinging open?

Yet, I never considered myself a parent. I had never given birth, never walked the floors with a fussy baby or been there for first steps and words. Step-parenthood is a gray designation that leaves you with one foot in each of the Mom/Not Mom camps. Thus, the difficulty in responding to a simple question about my parenting status.

When she was about 11, Angie and I were at the grocery store when the cashier smiled at her and said, "You look just like your Mom."

She smiled back and said, "Thank you." As we went out the door, Angie looked up at me and said, "Sometimes it's best just to go along, isn't it, Maggie?"

Yes, Sweetie, it is.

Happy Mother's Day to me.

A Very Barnes Christmas

"Did you clear the door yet?"

Bob was dragging the trunk of the evergreen into the living room. I was wrestling with the top half of the 15-footer and the answer was no, I was not yet inside the door.

We did it again. Cut down another beast of the forest to be the centerpiece of our Christmas celebration. It was our fifth holiday season on the hill, and our confidence was growing that we had developed a nearly infallible system to choose, cut and stand a majestic evergreen against the wall of glass that encases the front of our home.

We always did our reconnaissance trip in October, when the warmth of the autumn sun made selecting a tree comfortable. Gone were the days of freezing off various body parts until one of us gritted our teeth and said, "Yes, it does look like it's diseased, but we can cut that part out. Let's go."

This year, the crop had been bountiful, so we took our time and got a nearly perfect specimen. Waiting for us in the front room were the bucket, bricks, twine and sand that were the essential tools for securing the tree. While we had gotten much better at doing this over the years, I still felt trepidation as I pulled on my gloves and prepared myself for battle.

The system was deceptively simple: jam the stump of the tree into the bucket, stand the thing upright, use the bricks and sand to steady the tree in the bucket, tie the top portion to the ceiling beams and, when the seismic activity calmed, cut the rope binding the tree to itself.

My role in this operation also was easy - don't let the damn thing fall. It was my job to steady the tree by hanging on to the trunk while Bob locked it into place. Often, we resembled first-time Twister players, as he crawled around between my feet while I performed an awkward ballet, jumping over him and switching hands on the tree. We certainly never would win any style points, but we got the job done.

Conversation during this process is usually frowned upon, as we are both in deep concentration on our respective duties. What is said is not exactly poetic.

"No, your other left. My right!"

"Move your feet, Mags, I can't get…"

"Ow!"

"Sorry! The brick slipped."

"Are we back, ya know, toward the glass thing?"

"You mean the window?"

"Don't get snarky with me, pal. I'm being blinded by evergreen spears here."

"Tis the season to be impaled."

"Robert, you drop one more branch on my head and I will end you."

Fa, la, la, la, la, and all that.

This year, things were going suspiciously well. It's like when your toddler has been an angel for the entire church service, but you just know, come the sharing of the peace, he is going to spit up in the rector's hand.

The tree stood, accompanied by a chorus of our grunting, but the darn thing wouldn't stop. It went beyond vertical, continuing toward the windows, while Bob fought to control the weighted bucket with his foot.

"Too far! Bring it forward!"

I marshaled my remaining strength and shoved the tree back. What I couldn't see, through my sweat and needle-filled eyes, was that the tree, while colliding with the windows, had hooked its boughs behind the crucifix that adorned the center beams of the glass.

The cross was handed to me when I was 10 years old, on the day of my godmother's funeral. It had hung in every home I lived in since. It was simple by today's standards, just a brass cross with the figure of Jesus, encased in a wood frame. When we moved into this house, it fit perfectly on the wood beams of the front windows, and I felt secure with it watching over us.

The evergreen, clearly an atheist, had latched onto the cross and, when we brought the tree forward again, it ripped the crucifix from the beam and flung it into the air.

Bob and I, both helpless to do more than watch, wore the same panicked look as the cross performed a perfect mid-air somersault and crashed to the hardwood floor, skidding 8 feet into the foyer.

Silence.

A voice that vaguely sounded like mine whispered, "Oh no."

The tree began to shift again, and my attention was back on keeping my grip on it. I leaned around the greenness and found Bob looking back at me.

"This probably is not good," he panted. "Nothing like pissing off both Santa Claus *and* God."

"I've always wanted to spend Christmas in Belize," I shrugged, doubtful that we could ever outrun this batch of yuletide karma.

We tied the tree into submission and went to assess the damage to the cross. The wood was split all the way down the back and the brass section of the cross was bent. But the worst part was the fact that Jesus' left hand was nowhere to be seen.

"Well," Bob chirped, "at least it's not his right hand. You know how God is about that."

I elbowed him in the stomach with a glare. "Don't say things like that. We don't have insurance against a plague of locusts! You think Allstate covers bleeding walls? Don't think so! We're in real trouble here!"

A search commenced for the missing hand, but it only turned up two guilty looking felines. I shook a finger at them.

"Did you eat Jesus' hand?"

The cats shared a look that clearly questioned my mental stability.

"I bet it dropped down the floor vent," Bob said, peering into the dusty abyss of our heating system.

Whatever its fate, the left hand of our Lord and Savior was never recovered. Bob straightened up after another search attempt and looked at the tree, its boughs gracefully stretching as it settled into form.

"It's probably cursed now. Bet we come out in the morning and there's nothing but mounds of
needles on the floor. The tree will fling itself off the deck in remorse."

I do not take heavenly matters lightly, so I was soon in contact with our favorite member of the clergy, Father Hunter, for guidance.

"The tree did what?" Father's deep laughter filled my ear. "The heathen!"

"I know, I should have asked its denomination before bringing it home. They're natives of Germany, right? Maybe it's a Lutheran," I surmised.

Father roared again and then settled into his comforting, pastoral tone. "Maggie, God isn't nearly as concerned with these matter as we are. But for your own peace of mind, have the crucifix unblessed and then you can dispose of it with a clear conscience. The Lord doesn't want you losing sleep over this."

That's what we did and went on to have a wonderful holiday season.

93

There is a new cross in the front room this year. It's a little more modern than its predecessor, with a low profile design that hugs the beam it is gracing.

It does not have hands. I've got enough to explain when I get to Heaven.

The Family Tale

"Mags, you have to tell the garage story."

Family stories are universal. We all have them and they fall into two categories. There are those that showcase relatives at their finest; acts of great courage, intellect or devotion to mankind. And then there are those that suggest it is truly shocking that most of us manage to dress ourselves each day.

Welcome to the Holy Grail of category number two.

We had been married only six months. This simple fact does not alleviate me of any of the wrong doing to come, but it's a ploy for sympathy to claim the role of a newlywed. Please try to ignore the fact that I was far beyond the age of majority. Think "Gidget" and I will come out better.

At the time, my beloved was Chief of our city's fire department and a state fire instructor.

It was April, a month in the northeast that can contain scattered days of sunshine and warmth. This was not such a day. It was cool and overcast. As I tended to the dishes after dinner, Bob was headed to the garage. "The state sent me new turnout gear. I want to look at it."

Simultaneous to that statement, the phone rang. (Pay attention children and you will learn some history. Back then it was a wall-mounted device with a tethered system that only let you go so far.) It was my sister. I have two, the first friends I ever had in life and still incredibly dear to me and we like to talk.

Our garage was not attached to the house at that time. There was a space of maybe six feet between the back kitchen door and the one-car structure. It was an old building. Bobby raised the garage door, stepped into the darkened interior and started toward the large box next to the car. A moment later, the aging overhead door popped a spring, jerked off its tracks and slammed shut behind him.

You are already ahead of me here, aren't you? Well, stay with the tour. It's better than your imagination.

Bob could not lift the door without the mechanism being in place. No, there were no other doors in the garage. The only windows were the line of small panes in the door itself, facing the rear of the house. Through this glass he could clearly see into the kitchen.

After a moment of examining his situation, my ever-logical husband resigned himself to the fact that he was truly, completely, and inarguably trapped. No problem, he reasoned, for my bride of six months – remember that? – will come get me out as soon as she realizes what has happened.

This is as good a time as any to let you know that my husband was garbed in only a t-shirt and shorts. A minute turned into 15, then 30. As if the universe was taunting him, Bobby could see me, bathed in the warmth of the kitchen, steam from the dishwater still dissipating from the windows. I walked back and forth, phone firmly to my ear and mouth running like a Porsche 911.

He weighed his options. He could beep the car horn to get my attention. Then what? I had less chance of opening the door from the outside than he did. If he did catch my eye, what action would that result in? Calling the fire department? HIS fire department? "Hey Chief! (giggle) Need some help in there? (snort, guffaw) I'm glad we brought the camera. (hee-hee) You taught us how important documentation is. Smile!" Nope, a 911 call was not the answer.

Time rolled on. Pacing and analyzing can be strenuous activities, but they do not produce warmth. Bob's feet were icy and his legs were starting to tremble. He took the only action available to him. He broke the seal on the box from the Empire State and donned his professional uniform; bunker pants, turnout coat and boots.

Perhaps it was the act of dressing like a first-responder that reminded Robert of the only tactical advantage he had: the chainsaw.

Bobby cut a hole in the sidewall of the garage. I don't mean a modest hole that he could shimmy out of on his hands and knees. I mean a huge, gaping slash that Abraham Lincoln could have walked out of, complete with top hat.

How much would you have paid, dear reader, to be there when the blade of a chainsaw thrust out from *inside* the sealed garage and a fully dressed firefighter emerged?

Total time in the garage: one and a half hours.

Status of new wife: clueless.

Yes, I was still on the phone when Bob dragged back up the kitchen stairs, in his turnout gear, lugging the chainsaw. A fine layer of dust was splattered around the world's bluest eyes as he stared at me and said nothing.

I stared back in complete astonishment and confusion. Having no idea what had happened, I did make my only decent decision of the night and ended my conversation.

"Joanne, I have to call you back." I said with forced cheerfulness. I hung up and turned back to my silent husband. There was enough dead air between us to sing two choruses of "Stand By Your Man".

Then he spoke.

"Would you like to know where I have been for the last hour and half?"

"Sure, if you want to tell me." My voice sounded as thin as cheap vodka.

"I've been trapped in the garage."

"Oh."

(Give him two arms to cling to,
And something warm to come to
When nights are cold and lonely)

The scene before me made absolutely no sense and I was calculating like mad in my head. Of all the routes I could have taken, I went with, "Why are you wearing your turnout gear?"

"Because," he hissed through clenched teeth, "I…got…COLD!"

With that, he clunked his way back down the steps and out into the now dark night.

The evening ended in complete silence. He spoke not a word. We went to bed and the light was snapped off. I laid in the gloom, wondering if an annulment was still in play at the six-month mark and dreading the hassle with the DMV of changing my name back.

I felt a vibration and realized that his side of the bed was shaking. I leapt for the light and turned to find Robert in the throes of a classic case of silent laughter. Every inch of him shook, but there was yet no sound. A moment later, he erupted in a noise of pure glee and propped up on his elbows.

"I felt like such an idiot!" He roared. "I got laughing so hard I couldn't pull the starter cord on the chainsaw!" He spilled over like flood water for the next half hour; thinking about the fire department responding, scouring the garage for anything to use, watching me act like a teenager with a first phone while his toes went numb.

Visions of returning wedding gifts dissolved as my eyes watered from laughter. We settled down to sleep, holding hands.

As a coda to this epic family tale, when we built the new garage, Bobby included three, count 'em, three doors, multiple windows and what I suspect is an ejector platform to get out through the roof.

As for my phone call? I hit her back the next morning. We still had stuff to talk about.

Hey, I kept Bob in sight the whole time!

This Joint Ain't for Me

"Kiddo, we are out of options."

It's bad enough to hear those words from your plumber or the Electoral College, but hearing them from an orthopedic surgeon is a major bummer.

The dour man in the white coat turned the screen so I would have full view of my crumbling right hip. We had tried everything; physical therapy, injections, heat treatments and medication. But I hated the thought of losing some of my original equipment. I believe you should return to God at the end of your life with the same stuff He sent you out with. How else was I going to get my security deposit back?

"I'm too young for hip replacement," I pouted, but he shook his head. "You are right in the middle of the age spectrum. I've had 30-year-olds do this."

Probably cute, perky 30-year olds who took a week off from their zip-lining job to get a new hip popped in, did 20 laps in the therapy pool and got a low-fat something in a cup with extra foam on the way out the door. I, on the other hip, was a mid-50's grandmother who got winded watching the lightning round on "Jeopardy."

A blur of preoperative preparation later and it was the day of my surgery. Bob and I had attended "Joint Camp", an anxious gathering of my fellow sufferers, and had most of our questions answered. Our home went through its own prep, with the area rugs coming up, walkers and canes installed and the herd of cats lectured against "getting in Mommy's way."

With moments to go before my journey to the operating room, a charming nurse pushed "a little something to help you relax" into my IV port. Suddenly, the world looked like a Disney dream, complete with animation and musical score. The soap dispenser on the wall smiled at me, my Styrofoam slippers winked and Jimmy Durante stuck his head in the door and gave a thumbs-up. I have the foggiest memory of propping up on my elbows and questioning, "When did they stripe this room? It looks awesome!"

Bob turned to the nurse and said, "She's ready to go."

"Rehab" is a deceptively nice word for a painful process that hurts the body and frustrates the mind, but I was determined to regain my mobility as soon as possible. The primary purpose for the facility I was in was long-term care, so I did take pleasure in my designation as "the young one." That didn't stop the young activities director – I mean young, I have black dress shoes that are older – from trying to engage me in the daily fun.

"Hi Mrs. Barnes! Wow, you look wonderful today!" (I looked like death on a cracker, but the kid had a quota to meet.) "We are playing bingo today. Won't you join us?"

I declined, but suggested if someone kicked off a round of Texas Hold 'em, give a shout. "Deuces and Queens are wild, opening bid is two pairs of support stockings." She was not amused.

The only event I did roust myself out of my room for was a visit from the local animal shelter. I was having withdrawal from my kitties so a few minutes with a sweet Labrador was just what the veterinarian ordered.

Of course, I made several trips to the "exercise room", where a cheerful cast of therapists attempted to move my new hip via techniques I am quite sure the Geneva Convention had banned. They had an elaborate set-up to replicate the conditions we would be facing on the big day that we went home. There were stairs and doorways, couches and chairs. When Bob saw the kitchen mock-up, he told the therapist to skip that lesson with me. "Unless clinical studies have shown that replacement hips improve cooking skills?" I whacked him with my walker.

When your mobility is severely compromised, eating can become the highlight of the day. The food was good enough, but some of the menu selections brought forth an "Ummm…" more than a "Yummm…"

One day, my half-sheet of dietary delights included the following:

- Franks and beans, with Brussels sprouts
- Chipped beef over toast, with pickled beets
- Stuffed cabbage casserole

Good Lord. I'm trapped in a middle school in 1954! When the dietician came to pick up my menu, she said, "You haven't selected anything." I said, "Forgive me, but there is nothing on that summer camp menu I want to eat."

"You have to eat to recover from your surgery."

"No worries. I have activated the emergency culinary system. At this very moment, Seal Team Six is rappelling down the side of a pizzeria in an undisclosed location. In about twelve minutes, a flash bang is going to immobilize the nursing staff while the team breaches this window and hands me a large with pepperoni and extra cheese."

Health care workers can be so humorless. I bet they eat the food.

The pizza did appear as predicted, though in the hands of my dear friend Eleanor, who looked at my menu choices and shook her head. "And they wonder why old people are cranky," she said. The next night my husband secured his nomination as best spouse ever by showing up with my favorite entrée from a Valley restaurant.

Between a steady flow of contraband and the occasional lucky find on the menu, my cupboard was never bare.

I recovered fully and now enjoy setting off the theft alarms on my way into various stores while yelling, "Haven't had time to steal anything! It's just my hip!" Seriously. I now carry a card in my wallet to validate that part of my anatomy came, not from the mind of God, but from a factory in Warsaw, Indiana. Wonder if the vending machine there doles out chipped beef?

So, if joint replacement is in your future, fear not, I am here to help you plan. Have faith in your surgeon, bring comfy clothes, do your exercises, and pack a lunch. And a breakfast. And a dinner...

Getting Decked Out

"You know what would be nice?"

Bobby flipped down the top third of the newspaper and regarded me with the natural suspicion of husbands everywhere.

"What is that?'

"A small piece of flat land."

I was standing at the windows that offer a sweeping view of the New York-Pennsylvania border and our field and woods, all carpeted in snow and capped with a lead gray sky. Robert – a veteran of many encounters with my "ideas", simply waited.

"For a fire pit," I continued. "Wouldn't it be nice to have an outdoor fire pit? We just have too much slope." It was a fact that a portion of our acreage was at a steep enough pitch to cramp the legs of a mountain goat.

I sighed.

Now, back in middle school, when they took all the boys into one assembly to teach them to shave or belch or both at the same time, they put the girls together and introduced us to "female methods of persuasion." Some of these concepts cannot be discussed openly or I will lose my membership in the Sisterhood, but a couple of them exist in the public domain. Tears are the most commonly mentioned, but one of the go-to tactics in my toolbox is "the sigh."

It's gotta be impressive, starting from your knees. It should be sustained and loud enough to overcome environmental noise factors – like a husband with his fingers stuck in his ears. I am an expert sigher, and usually Bob knew all that was left was for the little timer to pop out of his goose in the oven.

However, men are not exactly weaponless themselves, and that moment at the window represented the last time I would be the lead dog on this particular home improvement project. In fact, all I did was kick the first stone off the mountaintop. The avalanche that followed was all on him. In a matter of hours, the simple idea of an eight-by-eight platform for a small fire pit had morphed into a tiered deck addition to the house, complete with outdoor kitchen, covered seating area and hot tub.

Staring at the architectural quality drawing my better half had produced faster than a hiccup, I realized I had played right into a plan that was fully developed in his head long before my sigh had begun its journey up my body.

We started gathering pieces of the deck project as we found bargains. The fire pit was an out-of-season snatch for a song and the stonework was a discontinued stroke of luck.

On a bitter March day, I saw a sale on the type of decking boards we were interested in. We trucked off the hill and found the stuff was just what we were after. We purchased just shy of a thousand square feet. (Remember my eight by eight idea? Forget it. All this thing was going to need was a windsock and the medical helicopter could land on it.)

"Will they deliver the boards?" I asked as I climbed back into the truck.

My husband grinned and shook his head.

"This," Bob said triumphantly, "is why we bought a trailer."

The autumn before, we picked up a 15-foot trailer, a nice one with sides and a gate, to help with all the chores our hilltop home seemed to necessitate. It was parked next to the garage, snoozing away the snowy days. Bob had the hitch set up on blocks, so it would be easy to back the truck up, fit the ball over the hitch, secure it and off you go.

Turns out, the blocks had shifted and the trailer was sitting firmly on the frozen ground. That was okay, because we had hydraulic jacks to lift the hitch back up and slide the blocks under again.

111

Bob retrieved the jacks and put one into position.

Crank. Crank. Crank. Crankity-crank-crank.

It sure looked to my untrained eye like the jack wasn't lifting anything, including my husband's spirits.

"It's too cold. No problem, " he rebounded.

The truck was turned on, the heat in the cab blasted and the unresponsive jacks placed on the seats.

One of us asked again about having the boards delivered. Instead, it was suggested by the other of us that all we had to do was prop the trailer up enough for me to jam the blocks back into place.

This was not suggested by me.

Bob got a 2x4, jammed it under the trailer hitch and pushed down while I tried to return the blocks to position.

THUD!

The trailer slipped off the board and crashed back to earth, triggering my self-preservation instinct. I leapt up and back and counted all my fingers upon landing.

"Ready to try again?" My husband showed no concern for my future ability to feed myself.

"Can't we just ask them what they would charge to deliver the boards?" I tried to sigh, but the cold had set up camp in my feet and no air was getting higher than my shins.

"For all those boards? It would be a fortune. Come on, give it another shot."

We did. This time, I got two of three blocks under the hitch before the trailer dropped again. We were painfully close. And by painfully, I mean frostbite.

"Bobby, it's one phone call. You don't have to ask, I will. I'm great at not knowing stuff. It's one of my best things!"

We had been at it for more than an hour. The lead sky was unloading an odd mixture of sleet and snow that plastered our faces and made breathing a contact sport.

The warmed up jacks were given another chance to be heroes, but declined to rise to the occasion. Finally, we got the trailer up high enough to receive the connection from the truck.

At the home improvement store, the first board was fed into the trailer and my husband dragged it in. In a heartbeat, we knew we had a numbers problem.

Fifteen-foot trailer. Sixteen-foot boards.

Bob did everything but stand on his head trying to get that board to fit. I looked at the mountainous pile of boards to be loaded, a trailer with a gate that couldn't be closed, and my half-frozen husband and decided to risk a question.

"Just for giggles," I said to the young man beside me, "what would you charge us to deliver this?"

"The boards? Up to your place?" The kid mentally calculated for about a Nano second, then responded.

"Twenty bucks."

Something deep inside of me snapped. It may have been my spinal cord when I whirled around with murder in my eyes and barked, "ROBERT!"

Informed of the delivery cost, Bob, still standing in the trailer with a half-bent board over his head, calmly replied, "Oh. Let's do that."

He was right about the size of the deck. He was right about the outdoor kitchen and the hot tub. He was right about the stone for the fire pit.

But the next time he won't ask about delivery, I'm skipping the sigh and going straight to the tears.

The Fall of a Great Baker

"You're cooking? Why?"

Even over the phone the look of horror on my stepdaughter's face was evident.

"I want to surprise Dad." I tucked the phone under my ear and continued my hunt for our largest mixing bowl.

"An attempt on his life will do it," she muttered and I pretended not to hear.

Fall Sundays, what is it about them? This weird nesting instinct comes over me like a pumpkin scent infused fog and I head for the kitchen. Despite a complete lack of training and a spotty track record of culinary success, each year I end up wearing an apron bedecked with leaves and humming "Tis a Gift to be Simple" while the November winds lash at the windows.

I must have been feeling especially Hallmark Channel-ish this year, because I was trying to bake a couple of things. I've often heard that people are either cooks or bakers, rarely both in one individual. I am neither, so I figure I've got an even shot at this. But, I must confess that Angie comes by her reticence honestly, as I fed her spoiled grape jelly when she was ten. Kid has the memory of an elephant.

(And I would like to point out that she had nary a case of strep throat that year.)

Pumpkin spice cupcakes. The recipe sat propped against the kitchen radio, surrounded by bowls, measuring cups and dry ingredients. I had reviewed the directions, like a new driver looking at the map before leaving the driveway and, though I had some questions, I felt confident this was a task even I was up to.

The act of baking is actually therapeutic and has been proven to lower your blood pressure. Or is it brain function? No matter. As I measured and stirred and hummed, my relaxed mental state brought about several deep, profound revelations, some of which I share with you now:

- Have you ever noticed how alike baking soda and baking powder look? Who thought that was a good idea?
- I separated the eggs, as instructed, but it was a pain to have to go to different rooms to retrieve them. Baking is certainly labor intensive.
- "Fold in with a spatula until there are no flour pockets" – What in the name of Julia Child is a flour pocket? It sounds like a bad thing. I base that solely on having never heard a cupcake described as being delightfully riddled with tasty flour pockets.
- A half-cup of brown sugar? I'd be happy to comply if this stuff wasn't one solid brick. What did I read about

bread keeping brown sugar soft? I wrapped a bag of bread slices around the brown brick and set it aside.

- How am I supposed to whisk something that clumps like boys at a junior high dance?
- "Add flour in two additions" – I hoped the new bath and guest room counted as two. I sure am trucking this bowl around a lot.
- This recipe is so narrow-minded. Something can be dense and fluffy at the same time – am I right? Of course I am.
- Here's an interesting tidbit; cream cheese is surprisingly aerodynamic for something that can cling to the ceiling.
- If you have bowls left over in your cupboard, you didn't do it right. I did it right.
- When tidying up after baking, it is best to start with the ceiling and work your way down with help from Mr. Gravity. Just a little tip from my kitchen to yours!
- I've heard of this "clean as you go" theory about baking, but where's the challenge in that? I prefer to see how high I can pile the pots and pans in the sink, sort of "kitchen-Jenga".

As I was waiting for the oven timer to ding, my niece Michelle called.

"I'm baking!" I offered cheerfully.

Michelle's voice dropped to a nervous whisper.

"What happened? Have you been kidnapped?"

"What?" I said. "What put that idea in your head?"

She breathed a sigh of relief. "I thought this was your secret panic phrase to tell me someone was holding you hostage."

Brat.

The cupcakes were supposed to be frosted with one of those decorating bags with the different tips on it. Stuff like that is not exactly standard equipment in our kitchen like say, a high-powered corkscrew or an industrial grade weather station that tells me when it's raining in Newfoundland. So, I just slathered about two inches of frosting on each cupcake and called it good.

My coworkers fell on those cupcakes like they never thought they'd eat again. And I'll have you know there were no reports of sudden onset stomach pain, fever or visual hallucinations.

If you factor in my hourly rate of pay at work and the cost of ingredients, those two dozen cupcakes cost $374.12. But can you really put a price on homemade love?

Pepto-Bismol, yes, but love, no.

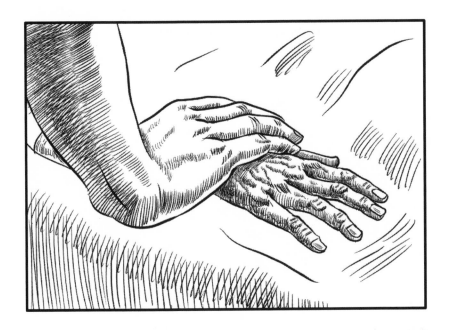

A Heartbreaking Gift

"I need you to do something for me."

I watched, barely able to draw a full breath, as my mother-in-law stared into my husband's face with painful intensity.

I could not fathom what he wanted to ask of her.

"She normally looks better than this."

That from Rosalie, my husband's mother, upon her introduction of me to visiting relatives.

Yep, I normally look better than I do early on a Saturday morning when I am not expecting company and I'm tackling a pile of laundry that looks like the Grand Tetons and a kitchen floor that could only be described as crunchy.

You had to know Rosalie Barnes to be nodding your head in total acceptance of the way she presented me. Just shy of 70 years old when I met her, Mom had a fierce countenance and set jaw that could frighten an IRS auditor. She was short on pleasantries. She expected things to be a certain way and when they weren't, someone was going to hear about it. There was no gray with Mom. If she liked you, you could find a clue here and there to confirm it. If she didn't like you, you knew it. Everybody knew it.

She was independent to a fault. Our daughter visited on a whim and found the 85-year-old on her knees, washing dishes in the bathtub. The sink faucet had been busted for a week, but she wasn't planning to tell anyone.

That self-reliant streak of hers was wound into every fiber of her being. We had a power outage after a summer storm and her small village was in darkness. I had taken her out to dinner and was insisting she return to our house to stay over.

"Why?" she had snapped.

"You have no lights," I reasoned.

"You think there's a spot in my house that I don't know after 60 years?" she reasoned right back.

She dragged her feet about leaving the restaurant, deciding on another trip to the salad bar and lingering over a dinner roll like it was a rare wine. I agreed to head towards her home, but stated without debate that if the power was still out, she was coming with me.

On the road to her place, I watched in astonishment as every house, farm and business we passed illuminated with the sudden return of power. Don't throw "coincidence" at me. Those electrons knew what was what.

When she was diagnosed with cancer, a mild-mannered lady turned up in her hospital room to talk to her about getting a wig.

"I don't need a wig," she said, jaw like granite.

"Mrs. Barnes, you have an aggressive treatment plan. I'm sorry, but your hair will fall out."

I swear to you, you could hear the gears in Mom's head locking into immovable position.

"No."

Flustered, the wig lady left the room.

She didn't lose one hair. Not. One. Hair.

Hers was a determination born of the Great Depression, a lifetime of work in the family business and a steadfast devotion to her community. So set in her ways was she, that when we got her some modern conveniences, she simply refused to acknowledge them. The cordless phone was left on the desk in the office while she went into the other room to check on the order. The microwave was used for storing her Tupperware. The copier/fax machine? Well, that wasn't going to dish the local dirt like the ladies at the post office, so forget it.

But even she had to yield to the intractable march of time. After my father-in-law died, she tried to keep the business going. She insisted on living alone, a demand that forced us to develop a secret network of informants around her to let us know when she needed help. (I still smile when I think of the furtive phone calls. Grown men whispering, "Don't tell her I told you but…")

Eventually she came to live with us. Battling illness and denied her independence, she faded into some ethereal, unreachable place between life and death. She hadn't spoken in days.

We took turns tending to Mom, talking to her with the full understanding that she was unresponsive and, despite her eyes often being open, would not really see us. I accepted what was happening with the comfort of my faith and the knowledge that we were making her as comfortable as possible.

Hers was a long, fulfilled life, indeed. But, like all families, we were greedy. We hoped for one more moment.

It was a Sunday, not long before Christmas, and the nurse had told us that we were getting near the end. When I rounded the side of her bed, Mom's eyes were open, and I could see that she tracked my movements.

"Hi, Mom," I whispered. "We're here with you."

She stirred, opened and closed her hands and lifted her arm. Her mouth moved. Bright eyes and a little sound from her and I rocketed back up the stairs, calling for my husband.

"Bobby! She's here! She knows! Hurry!"

When the sight of her only child came into view, Mom illuminated from somewhere deep inside. Her recognition of him was total. She raised her arms and enveloped him in the kind of hug only a mother could bestow.

It was early, not yet 6 a.m., and Bob hadn't stopped to throw on a shirt. I watched them and was overwhelmed by a sense of the circle coming around on itself. When he was born, Bobby was placed in her arms, wet and naked and crying. And now, all these years later, she cradled her son against her chest, tears on bare skin.

Hovering his face within inches of hers, Bobby told his mother that all was well, that the family was strong and she had made everything fine for us. There was nothing to worry about.

"Do one more thing for me, Mom," he asked, brushing her hair from her forehead.

"Go find Dad."

She passed that afternoon.

Everything is in readiness for Christmas. The monster tree has been wrestled into place. The wrapping is done and the menu is set. I'm sure it will be a lovely holiday with much laughter and wonderful surprises under the tree.

But no present will ever rival the one we were given on that frosty Sunday, when a loving mother and son gifted each other a sweet release to go on to what came next.

Can't Take That Cat Anywhere

"Where's Shadow?"

I didn't process my husband's question for a moment, as I was completely engaged in trying to decipher a recipe.

I understand cooking instructions about as well as the nuclear launch codes, but it was Thanksgiving weekend and I was determined to contribute something to our autumnal bounty.

"Shadow? I haven't seen him all morning," I replied while hacking away at a brick of brown sugar with a carving knife.

Shadow was our cat. Or rather, we were Shadow's humans. He ran the house and as long as that was clearly understood, we were free to meet his every demand. Shadow had lived on the streets until a bitter winter had him reconsidering his lifestyle choices. According to Bob, that's when he looked up and down the street for the people with the biggest L on their foreheads.

We met him in August. By October, he was laying on his back, snoring, in the center of our bed. Mission: accomplished.

Upon reflection, I realized I hadn't stepped over him in hours. A search was initiated and I immediately heard the concern in my husband's voice when he announced, "Here he is."

Shadow was in Bob's closet, crammed into the farthest corner he could reach. My heart dropped when I saw the clouded look in his eyes. I crawled toward him and extended my hand. Instead of the cheek rub and throaty purr I had come to love, he was still and silent. Something was wrong.

Bob leaned in and got hands on him, drawing him slowly forward with gentle words of reassurance. When the cat came into the light, the problem became clear. One side of Shadow's face was bloated out so far he could only squint with that eye. His fur bore a long, angry-looking slash mark that parted the perfect black sheen of his coat.

Bob tilted Shadow's head as gently as possible and whispered, "Who'd you get this from, Shad?" The lump was warm to the touch, an infection for sure. As a former resident of the streets, Shadow had learned to defend himself and usually gave better than he got when he tangled with a fellow feline. But this round would go to his opponent.

Remembering the holiday weekend, I called our vet's office with little hope of a response. Sure enough, I got a recorded message, directing me to call the emergency vet in another town. After a description of what we were facing, the Vet said, "Yep, sounds like he's got an abscess. Can you get him here?"

"Here" was twenty miles up the interstate, but there was no discussion. Of course we were going.

I cradled Shadow in my arms without resistance and felt a stab in my heart when he just lay motionless, no meow, no leaning into me in affection. He was one sick kitty.

"Do you want the carrier?" Bob was putting on his jacket, one foot heading to the cellar stairs, but I shook my head.

"He doesn't have the strength to go anywhere," I answered. "I'll just hold him."

"This will be the first long drive in the new car," Bob mentioned as we went out the door.

The new car was a beauty, a Jeep Grand Cherokee that Bob had brought home less than a week ago. It was midnight blue with gray interior and rode like you were sitting on the living room couch. We joined a steady traffic flow of holiday travelers. Shadow was still as a statue in my lap, showing none of his usual curiosity about his surroundings. My husband and I spoke softly to each other, the concern for our beloved pet hanging heavy between us. We had only gone ten miles when I felt a strange sensation of warmth on my leg. The next moment brought a downright uncomfortable feeling of something wet. I shifted Shadow a few inches to investigate my left leg and was startled into immobility by what I saw.

131

Shadow's abscess had ruptured. The vicious claw mark from his adversary had opened and bright green goop was pouring from his face onto my jeans.

"Bobby! Look!" I had found my voice and was trying not to frighten the animal in my lap, while simultaneously spurring the man next to me to do something. Anything.

Bob managed to keep the Jeep in the lane while stealing glances at my predicament. A second later, my problem became our problem when the smell of the cat's infection ballooned in the vehicle. (Marriage is all about sharing, you know.)

Think of the most vile, putrid thing you have ever smelled. Think of the time you accidently left a gallon of milk in the trunk of the car in June and you didn't find it until August. Or when your son came home at Christmas and opening his duffle bag confirmed for you that he had yet to find the laundromat at college. You could bottle that and call it perfume in comparison to what, by now, had filled the interior of the Jeep. I was fighting a losing battle to contain both the cat and the slime on my lap, rather than let it contaminate the interior of the new car.

"Do we have paper towels?" I was hissing at my husband through clenched teeth, in an effort to not breathe through my nose or open my mouth too much.

"Not so much as a Kleenex," he responded.

For his part, Shadow had sat up straighter and was showing signs of life. In fact, the lessening pressure on his face was making him feel so much better that he decided to hurry the process along by rocking his head back and forth. Quickly.

Streams of the green stuff flung around the cabin, hitting the dashboard, the roof, the side windows and me. Bobby, benefitting from a life spent in emergency response, managed to duck and dive around the bombardment, all the while keeping us in the center of the road. It was as if his body had gone into a serpentine pattern – moving targets and all that. He was making fish-like movements with his mouth and, I felt sure, thinking longingly of his firefighting gear in the back.

I was desperate to get the cat to sit still. "Shadow! No!" I held him tighter and felt the sticky gunk seep deeper into my sleeves. I considered opening a window but was too fearful of Shadow deciding he no longer needed medical attention and jumping. My eyes began to water and my Eggos were gonna leggo of my intestinal tract in another minute.

My husband and I looked at each other in that special, unspoken language of long-time couples. My message to him was, "I don't care if they ban you from owning as much as a skateboard for the rest of your life. Do whatever you have to do to get to that Vet's office."

The marriage mind-meld was intact, for a moment later the Jeep started eating pavement like a hobo on a hotdog. I think we took the final turn on two wheels and screeched to a stop at the door of the animal clinic. In dismay, I counted six other cars already parked.

When we walked in the door, Shadow now ruining the front of Bob's favorite leather jacket, it was their noses, both human and animal, that turned every head to us. A cloud of green air floated around us. My jeans were blackened and shiny, hair matted, jacket sleeves bearing evidence of an apparent battle with a vat of pistachio pudding.

All was silent. When the door opened and the assistant questioned, "Who's next?" every finger came to us.

Shadow survived that day – and many more battles – to live out his years with us.

Since then, Barnes family tradition dictates that every new vehicle is christened with floor mats, an atlas, disinfectant, rubber gloves, a level 2 hazmat suit, and paper towels. Lots of paper towels.

A Stranger Amongst Us

"Bobby? Look!"

It was one of those summer Friday afternoons that sends the Chamber of Commerce running for the camera and the inhabitants of cubicles inching towards the door. The sky was sapphire blue and cloudless. The breeze was singing in the trees and my mood was as sweet as the fragrant air. Until I saw the person.

Bob raised his eyes from the pair of dress shoes he was polishing and glanced down into our field. From the far corner of the woods strode a figure.

Now, I am usually a very friendly person. I'll strike up a conversation with just about anyone. My mother said I would have made a horrible toll taker. (It was a job, children, Google it.) Instead of moving traffic along, I would have chatted up drivers about what souvenirs they bought and admired their photos.

Since our move to the hilltop, however, I have developed a protective nature about our little compound. A private road with four houses makes for a predictable traffic pattern and even an unfamiliar car going by raises my defenses.

My husband, who is infuriating in his constant state of calm, will say, "It's a car, Mags. They've been around awhile now."

"Yes," I reply with eyes squinted in suspicion, "but up here they're either lost or looking for trouble."

"Probably casing the joint," Bob offers as he hits the button on the coffeemaker. "Your collection of vintage Tupperware would fetch a handsome price on the black market."

Sometimes I think that man does not take me seriously.

Back to that Friday. I'm always up for company, but this person was coming out of the woods, our woods, onto our property, unknown and uninvited. And he was waving a...tennis racket? Leaning as far over the deck railing as I dared, I could see him – for it was a he – striding across our field like he was sorry he was late and waving a tennis racket in front of his face nearly constantly.

"Bobby, why is he coming here? What does he want? And why in the name of sanity is he waving that racket around?"

My better half stopped brushing the toe of his wing tips long enough to say, "Those are all excellent questions, my dear. I assume we will get them answered when he gets here." Then he resumed brushing, as if it were the most natural thing in the world for a stranger to be charging across our field, armed, and with unknown intentions.

"But, aren't you going to stop him? We don't know what he's going to do!"

Bob glanced over the railing again.

"Not much with that backhand."

To my rising concern, the stranger had reached the bottom of our tractor road and started up it. This thing is not exactly a public access route. It is the path Bob takes to get the John Deere into the field for mowing. There is only one place it goes...our house. A scant 150 yards separated us from... whoever he was. Being totally incapable of just standing there and waiting, I took the only action I felt was appropriate.

"Hello!" I called down from the deck with forced warmth. "Won't you have some wine?"

My strategy here was two-fold; 1) He was now aware that we were aware of him coming, a fact that may give him pause if he intends to pummel us to death with said tennis racket and, 2) if he carries out his murderous plot anyway, he will feel great remorse over killing such a polite lady. Cagey, I know.

"Ya got a beer?"

Well, what do you know? He doesn't want to risk a headache from the nitrates messing with his ability to remember an alibi after the police find our bodies. Before I could respond, Bobby was on his feet and heading towards the fridge.

"Robert!" I hissed. "What are you, the waiter? We're not entertaining this person. Go out there and find out what he wants first."

I felt bad for sending the love of my life out to face a potential serial killer, but I do recall those sorts of duties being assigned to him during our wedding vows. It was right after killing snakes and letting me put my ice block feet on his back when I get into bed. The two men came face-to-face in the driveway and shook hands. I sat on the deck with "9-1-" punched into my phone and watched breathlessly.

Well, the whole thing turned out fine. His name was Mark and his family was the original settlers of the hill. His son was going to build on the land below ours, and Mark thought he'd better come up and apologize in advance for any trouble it caused us. The racket turned out to be a bug zapper, increasing my relief at not being bludgeoned with it because the constant "Zzzzt!" would have driven me mad while I bled out.

We had a lovely chat and the men worked one of their "deals" where not much gets said, but all that is unspoken is understood. The masculine version of "wink, wink, nudge, nudge" and suddenly we had the okay to trim back some trees that weren't really ours as long as we didn't get too picky about our boundary pins in the woods. To be honest, I couldn't really follow how we got to an agreement, but an hour later it was all handshakes and smiles and Mark trooped back down the tractor road and off into the woods, racket swinging and zapping the whole way.

"See?" Bobby moved back to his chair and examined his sparkling dress shoes. "Not all strangers are enemies. You should relax more."

Good advice. I will relax.

Just as soon as I count my Tupperware.

I Can't Cook - Don't Ask Me

"Mom? I need to tell you something."

My mother's eyes shifted from the ceiling of her hospital room to me. The oxygen mask covered most of her small face, but her raised eyebrows told me she was listening.

Mom had been hospitalized many times in her later years, but this visit had a weighty feel to it that made us certain we were coming to the end of her life.

"I want to talk to you about Bob."

Mom had only met Bobby once, so it was with trepidation that I chose to tell her this news as we faced the prospect that she would never come home again.

"I'm going to marry him, Mom. You don't have to worry about me anymore. He loves me and he will take great care of me. Do you understand? Is this okay with you?"

Her face brightened and I saw a flash of the smile that had warmed my soul from my earliest memories. She suddenly struggled and I helped her rise up on her elbows. When her hand was free, she pulled the oxygen mask from her face. I felt the pulse of cool air from it, heard the hissing sound rush by and I braced myself. She had made a herculean effort to speak and I knew the loving words she was about to bestow would live in my heart forever.

"Marry him," she gasped. "Or you will starve to death."

It may not have been the sum of all worldly wisdom, but it was the ultimate proof of how well my mother knew her baby girl.

I can't cook. I can't sew. I can clean a house but it is a long and clumsy process, devoid of the brilliant shortcuts or pearls of hidden wisdom often handed down by female ancestors.

I once left a watermelon on the kitchen floor so long that it fused to the linoleum and had to be amputated like a Civil War soldier's leg. I thought irons were doorstops that heated up for some unfathomable reason. Occasionally, I still pray for Mary Alice, who finished the required A-line dress that got me through sixth grade Home Ec. (I hadn't made a large enough hole for my head. Who thinks of details like that?)

To the Martha Stewarts of the world, I am known as "She whose name is not mentioned."

When I moved into my first apartment, my mother gifted me a microwave. Upon opening the door, dozens of grocery coupons and recipe cards cascaded onto the floor at my feet. By the time I met my husband, I had cultivated a solid diet based on the four major food groups: microwave, take-out, crockpot and dinner-dates. I could handle recipes if the most complicated step was "apply heat to contents." As my best friend at the time routinely asked me, "So, what did you dump out of a box tonight?"

There are legions of tales about my lack of domestic prowess, but when I think about my mother, it always comes back to the episode that made her laugh the hardest I ever heard her in my life.

I was in high school. It was an early day of summer vacation and I couldn't find a pair of shorts that appealed to me. Sorting through my wardrobe in the time honored teenage method of flinging things on to the floor behind me, I came across a discarded pair of jeans. A light bulb went on over my head. It was held aloft by Daisy Duke.

I bounced down the stairs and into the dining room, equipped with the jeans and a huge pair of scissors. I cleared the table and laid the jeans out. A contemplative moment followed while I selected the perfect length and seconds later, I was in possession of the world's cutest pair of cut-off shorts. I could already envision the lustful double take of the cute boy across the street. This summer would be epic.

I bounded back up the stairs for a fitting, during which time my mother and my sister Joanne returned to the living room from a late morning cup of tea on the porch.

When I came back down the stairs, I am sure my mother heard the true befuddlement in my voice. "Mom? What's the problem with this?"

I rounded the foot of the stairs and stood before the ladies with the world's cutest cut-off shorts…pulled all the way up to my chest. The denim strands dangled near my belly button and below them sat my pink Jockey Girl underwear. The look on my face conveyed the sincere confusion of a total, unapologetic idiot.

There was silence in the house, as I slid the shorts up and down the length of my body, unabated. When I raised my head, my mother and sister were staring at me the way scientists gaze upon a lesser species of animal who spends hours fascinated by its own big toe.

In the next heartbeat, my family exploded in laughter, hard, loud laughter that made coherent speech impossible. My sister took a step toward me, but had to lean against Mom for reinforcement while the two of them howled.

It is pathetic to say, but I was now confused times two, once by the illogical behavior of the shorts and now, by this bizarre, albeit united, reaction.

My mother's funny bone had one telltale sign of full activation. She would have to take her glasses off to wipe her flowing eyes. At the sight of me, she removed them and her face rested in her other hand while her entire body shook.

Joanne finally mustered enough strength and oxygen to gently inform me, "Mags, you cut above the crotch. Those aren't shorts anymore."

Hearing the situation put into words seemed too much for my mother, who erupted in fresh waves of hilarity and dropped her head onto her crossed arms on the table. Joanne reached across the table and lifted up the remnants of the jeans.

"Didn't you..." Jo paused to gasp and tried to straighten her aching sides. "Didn't you think it was odd that the legs were still connected?" She offered the jeans, legs still latched together below my less-than-surgical incision.

Ohhhh....

The "shorts" made a cameo appearance at my 40th birthday party, thanks to sisters who retain things as well as Bill Gates' iPhone. Shortly after that, they mysteriously disappeared. My neighbors reported some late digging one foggy night around the same time, but I'm not convinced there's a connection.

The tomatoes were huge this year, weighing down the plants in our garden. They were round and chubby with ruby flesh. I picked a half dozen and sliced them thinly. The preheated pie crusts were filled, and then I added sea salt, cracked black pepper, basil and trimmed scallions. I brushed on a layer of mayo and cheddar cheese. When the oven timer dinged the pies came out bubbling with subdued colors of red and orange and deeply tanned crust.

For a moment, the kitchen was still and quiet. Then a sudden lift of air blew by the house, encouraging the wind chimes to dance with the music of cathedral bells. I swore I heard her voice.

"Well done, baby girl! Just stay away from the scissors!"

The Sounds, or Lack Thereof, Love

"Hearing aids? Me?"

I took a deep breath and kept my voice calm, just like the intervention book advised.

"Yes, sweetheart, my love. I believe you are having just the tiniest trouble hearing."

"What?"

He went, unhappily, but he went, and got a set of small units that sat comfortably in his ears. They helped greatly, with one drawback. When he ate, Robert felt like he was locked in a washing machine that had been fed broken glass. The chewing was loud.

But, we were starting to have more of these discussions, two decades into our marriage. I was suddenly squinting at small print, the first step on that blurry path to getting optical assistance. Bob was having some dental issues, including one recent busted tooth that resulted in his spot-on impression of Sylvester the cat. I had developed the most disturbing habit of...how shall I say this...not exhibiting perfect bladder control when engaged in extreme activities like laughing hard. Or sneezing. Or...don't give me that look! After age 50 everything that was tight sags, things that were loose go stiff and everything else heads south like a duck in winter and doesn't come back. You got an issue with it? Talk to God. It's His design.

Anyway…one night at a restaurant, Bob opted to take his hearing aids out during dinner with his Mom and me. As he reached around to tuck them into his jacket, which was hanging on the back of his chair, they bounced out of his hand and on to the floor. In one of those cosmic episodes of perfect bad timing, the largest waitress in the county walked over the tiny devices and crushed them into ten gazillion pieces.

Bob snapped his head up and looked at me in utter disbelief. The waitress strode on, unaware that she had just ground $5,000 of our limited funds into the carpet. My husband, trying to keep the disaster from his mother, attempted to pick up the shattered segments of hearing aid, but it was like trying to sweep dust into your hand. It was hopeless.

It was a quiet dinner on multiple fronts. Bob was furious with the freak accident, Mom was unaware of the situation and I, forgive me, was trying not to laugh. What are you going to do, right? I knew Bobby would find it funny, too. Eventually. Hopefully, before he could track down the business card of that divorce attorney we met on vacation last year.

Stifling another giggle and avoiding my husband's tortured face, I was looking around the restaurant when a meatball leapt off my fork as if spring-loaded and bounded down my white blouse like a snowboarder. The resulting tic-tac-toe pattern was brilliant red with a greasy sheen. My mother-in-law raised an eyebrow and asked if I was breaking in a new mouth. Robert looked like a man coming to the realization that he is trapped in a low-budget sitcom without a laugh track. The giggle began another determined hike up my throat. I got to the ladies room before I had to use the facilities, but it was very close. I cleaned up my shirt as best I could and we headed home.

In the car with my enraged spouse, my stained blouse and my clueless in-law, I was holding together pretty well. Then it happened.

"You two are awfully quiet tonight. Is something wrong?" Mom chirped from the backseat.

"What?" said Bobby.

I chewed on the inside of my lip and rapturously studied the passenger side scenery, but I was fighting a losing battle not to burst into raucous laughter and/or pee my pants. Possibly both.

We got Mom home and headed to our street in silence. It was all I could do to breathe. I felt like I had clamped every opening in my body shut, including my mouth. My vision was getting wavy. The moment the door was open, I rocketed for the bathroom, but not without a drop or two of collateral damage.

When I emerged, I knew I must have been a sight. My pants were off and I was carrying my tomato-stained blouse.

My husband was standing in the middle of the kitchen, gazing sadly at the mashed hearing aids cupped in his hands.

I extended the blouse to him. "Can you see what water temperature I should wash this in?"

There was complete silence in the house, punctured only by the ticking of the kitchen clock, seemingly giving wings to our rapidly disappearing youth.

His face went pale, then flushed like an atomic sunrise.

"Good God, Maggie!" he roared. "I knew we were going to grow old together. But I didn't realize it would be by Thursday of next week!"

With that he tossed the busted plastic in the trash, snatched the blouse, pretreated in and threw it in the wash and stomped to the bedroom.

I followed him and leaned against the bedroom door and finally did what I had tried my damndest not to do for two hours. I laughed. Out loud. Hard. Giggled, snorted, chortled, the whole thesaurus. I wiped my eyes and composed myself only to collapse against the door again and howl.

And my beloved husband, with whom I find the thought of eternity not nearly long enough, gave me one of the greatest gifts ever.

He laughed.

Then I ran for the bathroom.

A Grateful Heart

"Thank you, God."

The gravel crunched in the driveway and the noise from the truck's engine wafted into the kitchen windows on a spring breeze. For a moment, I felt rooted to the floor, like my legs would have betrayed me if I had taken a step. I folded the dishtowel I was holding, laid it on the counter and bowed my head in relief.

Another emergency attended and he was home.

There was no ambiguity about it when the minister said, "Do you take this man?" When I raised my eyes and looked at Robert, I saw the face of the finest person I'd ever known. He was so handsome, standing tall in the dark blue dress uniform of his chosen profession - the fire service.

No, there was no way I could have missed what I was truly agreeing to on that October evening. Bobby and his groomsmen were all in their dress uniforms, gleaming gold badges and five-striped sleeves indicating the rank of Chief of Department. We left the church on the most expensive bridal limo ever, a fire engine. Our wedding cake, designed by the groom, sported little red helmets and toy fire trucks.

I knew what marrying a Fire Chief meant.

Our home revolves around his job. There are scanners and pagers throughout the house that crackle with calls day and night. Family dinners are choreographed around the radio traffic. Everyone is engaged in conversation, and then the scanner tones out that certain melody and the table falls silent. No one breaks rhythm eating, but all talking ceases. Depending on the nature of the call, the following moments are filled either with a boisterous return to the conversation, or a hasty last few bites, and the shoving back of chairs.

Emergencies have no respect for the calendar. Bobby gets called out on holidays, vacations, and more than once, anniversaries. As I told a friend, "If we're having the worst argument or the best sex, if the radio says he goes, he goes."

Bad weather presents situations ripe for accidents, fires and medical emergencies, so while the rest of the community hunkers down with family and hearth, my husband is heading out. I knew all of this. I accepted all of this. But, for the decades I have spent in a front row seat to my husband's career, I have never fully conquered the worry.

Like all spouses of emergency responders, I knew what could happen. We watch the national reporting of firefighter deaths. We rejoice over the "close calls", which resulted in no injury, but a great story to tell. And we weep with our fire service family when the worst happens. At every firefighter's funeral, I glue my eyes to the widow. Every one of us knows, there, but for the grace of God…

We are not unique. Among the minority of the population that protects the majority, this story could be applied to any responder. Volunteer or paid, urban or rural, they all leave their loved ones to safeguard someone else's family.

Bob does get himself into some jams. He happened by the river one April morning in time to see a man wading into the water, intent on killing himself. Bobby plunged in after him and fought him back to the shore, holding him out of the water until help came. He advanced a hose line through the front door of a burning home, and dropped straight through the weakened floor. One night, as we were getting in the car for a dinner out, the tones dropped for a house fire in our neighborhood. I got back out of the car and Bobby took off like a shot. I knew he would go to the scene first, rather than the station, as we were the closest.

A man on the front lawn told him he was not sure if everyone was out of the house. So, alone and with no equipment, Bob went in to search. Have you ever tried to make your way around an unfamiliar house blindfolded? That's what firefighters do – with the added challenges of heat, smoke and fumes. The rear stairs took an odd turn near the bottom, and Bob fell. Despite his injury, he dragged himself out the back door and forced himself to his feet. He could hear the sirens getting closer and knew he had to be ready to command the fire ground.

I listened to him do just that for two hours on the scanner and was dumbfounded when he crawled in our door, unable to stand. It took weeks for him to recover from the leg injury. My fear about what had happened turned into rage when it was revealed that the man who was in front of that burning house was the person who had started the fire. He watched my husband run in, unprotected, knowing full well that no one was inside. I wanted to take a sledgehammer to the idiot myself, but Bobby was unfazed. It was part of the job.

Not that the job doesn't come with some non-traditional perks, it does. For instance, we once educated an entire hotel lobby full of people about the fact that a ladder truck cannot reach higher than the fifth floor in most hotels. Then had the fun of watching the front desk deal with a dozen requests to change rooms.

Children look at a firefighter in uniform and instantly see a hero. One day in front of the firehouse, two brothers were walking to school too fast for their little sister to keep up. Watching from the doorway, Bob walked out to the little girl and, offering his hand, escorted her past her awestruck brothers to the bus stop.

We once traveled to Buffalo to attend the funerals of two firefighters who were killed in the line of duty. We were in a fire department

159

vehicle and, right from the toll booth on the Thruway to the restaurant we ate in, our money was no good. People driving by waved, held up the peace sign, or mouthed "Thank you" as they passed. The fact that we didn't know the heroes who died meant nothing. They were our brothers.

So when he comes home every night, it is a celebration of sorts for me. Fire wives are advised to "trust his training." I do, but it does little to lessen the knot in my stomach each time he leaves. I know that even when all precautions have been taken, fate still deals the final card. Sometimes, things just happen. It is a fear that hangs in my brain like a dark fog whenever he is out of sight.

This essay is a tribute to all the Bobs out there who do what they do for the love of the job and their community. It is also a salute to those who wait for their Bob to come home. The spouses who handle the kids solo. The children who feel the ache of that empty chair during the school play or soccer game. You are not alone. We are bound together by our shared dedication to helping our loved one do what they do best.

May all of them always come home.

Trimming the Tree

"It's gone?"

There are rhetorical questions like, "Is it raining?" when your slightly damp friend comes in. Then there are rhetorical questions like, "It's gone?" when you are looking at your spouse across a yawning abyss in the ground where an evergreen tree was supposed to be.

Robert, the crown prince of understatement, responded with, "It would appear so."

My shock quickly gave way to anger.

"Somebody stole our Christmas tree!"

"Stole" was probably too strong a word, as we hadn't technically paid for it yet. But we did adorn the spruce with fluorescent yellow strips of plastic, each bearing our last name, in the proud tradition of tree-taggers throughout the millennia. Lots of yellow streamers. That thing looked like a unicorn at its tenth birthday party.

"Who steals a tagged Christmas tree?" I demanded of the gray skies above the farm. "That's a puppy-kicker for sure. Anyone who steals a tree is an orphan-beating, nun-insulting, puppy-kicker!"

Bob hiked an eyebrow. Living with me, that eyebrow gets a workout. He really should attach his Fit Bit to it.

Whatever my opinion of the low life scum that took our tree, we were faced with the same dilemma. It was already the second week of December and we, a family famous for their yuletide festivities, were without a tree. An extensive search of the tree farm was undertaken. I was half-hearted about it. This was the holiday equivalent of going to the prom with your second choice. I was going to make the best of it, but I was not happy.

We found a tree that was acceptably lovely and near to 14 feet tall, a prerequisite for making the cut, so to speak, for our home. As usual, it took the two of us to pull it out into the road the farm folks had plowed around the rows of trees. In fact, it took the two of us and two of them. And a sled. Pulled by a four-wheeler. Truth is, it was one of the harder extractions I could recall. I was sure it was my frustration with the day that was draining my strength.

Once home, we attempted our usual dragging of the tree through the front door. It barely moved. We took a little break, held on tighter and pulled harder. It came this time, but we were both breathless with exertion before we cleared the foyer.

Straightening up, Bob gasped, "This thing has to weigh 300 pounds." Having never tried to lift 300 pounds before, I had to take his word for it.

We looked at the cleared spot in the front room, looked at the evergreen and looked at each other. Bob shook his head in resignation and said, "We're gonna need mutual aid."

For those of you who grew up in non-EMS families, allow me to elaborate. Mutual aid is the term used when a fire department is facing a situation that requires more staffing and equipment than they can throw at it. The surrounding departments bring their people and stuff and together they work on solving the problem. Bob loves mutual aid as an emergency response tactic. He hates it when it comes to asking for help at home.

So we made some calls and pals Derrick and Rob were the only idiots…I mean, *dear friends*, who actually answered their phones. Standing in the foyer, the two of them tugged at the tree and gave us a look that said, "How did you ever think…?" I told them I had never had a hernia and wanted to try one out.

I did some guiding and some pushing, but the menfolk did all the heavy lifting. What looked to be a nice, full evergreen in the forest had rapidly become dense and impenetrable in our living room. By far, it was the heaviest tree we ever had brought home, and we all breathed easier once it was in place and restrained with yards of high-gauge fishing line.

We had missed noticing that the shape was not as ideal as we would have liked. (I told you my heart was not in it!) In fact, several branches poked out oddly on all sides, giving the tree a disorganized look that hardly jived with "peace on earth." Bob keeps a pair of heavy-duty clippers on hand for matters such as this, and I handed them to him. But he shook his head and started up the stairs for the garage.

That is when I started to worry.

My apprehension was justified when my beloved pushed back through the door with the hedge trimmers - the massive, powerful, meant-for-outside-use-only hedge trimmers, complete with 40 feet of orange industrial extension cord. Nat King Cole was trying to tell us about Jack Frost nipping our body parts, but the roar of the trimmers drowned him out. It was a surreal juxtaposition to view the silent gentleness of the snowfall and the serenity of the Holy Family nestled in the manger, all the while dodging branches that were ricocheting around the room.

"Yuletide carols being sung by a…"
"Look out!"
"VROOOOMMMMM!"
"Watch your head!"
"…and folks dressed up like…"
"Incoming!"
"VROOOOMMMM!"

While I buried my face behind a couch pillow, Derrick and Rob were having a delightful time, catching severed tree parts in mid-air and directing Bob to the spots that were still asymmetrical. They were snapping photos of the operation, praising Bob's carving skills and admitting that they had never thought of bringing power tools to such a mundane task. (To the women in their lives, I now apologize, belatedly, but sincerely.)

Once the tree was declared "even," the guys helped us clean up the wreckage of my living room, shake the remnants out of the trimmer and wind up the neon orange cord. Which was good, as the clash with red and green was making my head hurt. Thanks and handshakes all around and our helpers were heading for the door.

Rob did make a point of saying that whenever we were planning to get our tree next year, he was busy that day.

But all in all, it was a grand night for mutual aid.